pattern of sand (through lace) +
neg. space

FREYA STARK

ARABIAN   DESERT

text in
white   FREYA

LOUISE BOYD

colours +
shore of
landscape/
clothes.

GREENLAND

GABON

GABON

pattern in lace
(three lines) & same
pattern
on
islands

EVELYN

text on
top

POLYNESIA

POLYNESIA

EVELYN
cheeseman

NEIL ARMSTRONG

The MOON

The MOON
NEIL ARMS
TRONG

Illustrators'
Sketchbooks

Martin Salisbury

Contents

Introduction

As a species, illustrators tend to be rather timid, retiring creatures – shunning attention and, like small furry mammals, occasionally emerging from their studio-burrows and blinking at the daylight. Although their reproduced work is often consumed and enjoyed by large audiences, they are not generally required to be present to witness it. Moreover, the process that underpins and nurtures the visual 'voice' that speaks from the page or screen usually remains unseen as well. For the professional athlete or musician, those endless hours devoted to hitting tennis balls, pounding the streets, practising scales or fine-tuning the singing voice are an accepted part of the route to success. The old adage of 'practice makes perfect' may be somewhat glib, but it does serve to remind us that there is a great deal more to an artist's effortless-looking final image than meets the eye – literally as well as metaphorically. When it comes to the visual arts, however, perfection is a tricky concept.

But the sketchbook for the illustrator is not just a practice ground. Although on the face of it the connection between the sketchbook and the wider, more familiar visual vocabulary of the individual illustrator would seem to be an obvious one, the many and varied attitudes and approaches to be found in the personal testimonies and within the pages of the semi-secret sketchbooks of the artists featured in this book tell us otherwise. For some, the sketchbook is a comfort zone, a place where drawings, notes and shopping lists can be unselfconsciously scribbled without fear of judgment. For others, it may be the home of methodical research and information-gathering, a 'suitcase of ideas', or a place where speculative experimentation without a conscious end goal can be indulged. Some of the artists in this collection use their sketchbooks entirely for drawing directly from observation, while others rarely, if ever, draw from life at all.

Then there is the psychology of the sketchbook: the seductive appeal of a brand-new, unopened sketchbook, leading to fear of that first blank page and the consequent danger of self-conscious mark-making. And the boundaries between 'sketchbook', 'notebook' and visual journal can often be blurred – many artists (among them Ronald Searle) combining drawing, sequential storyboarding, scraps of stimulating visual ephemera, newspaper articles, colour charts and material lists, all within the pages of the same book.

The number of illustrators who fall into the category of 'digital natives' – in other words, belonging to the generation of people whose adult lives have been lived in the familiar company of digital media – increases daily. Whether or not they are working fully or partially on-screen, they have grown used to the 'safety net' that Photoshop provides: the knowledge that anything and everything can be changed or corrected. This has been, in many ways, liberating – an escape from the fear of failure. But it can also lead to missed opportunities to appreciate and learn from the happy accidents that are too often instinctively obliterated before they have been reflected upon. We could of course describe the iPad as, for some illustrators at least, a digital sketchbook. The vast majority of illustrators today, however, still seem to value the physical sketchbook as the home of research and drawing, and as a convenient receptacle of visual thoughts before they slip away. The physical nature of these often battered, much-handled artefacts forms an important record of the thought processes of the illustrator, just as the various frantically scribbled drafts of an original music score provide such valuable insight into the gradual development of a composition.

For the outsider, a glimpse into these private worlds can be fascinating, and often surprising. For academics and students in the field of illustration, they can often be far more revealing than the published, 'tip of the iceberg' illustration work.

A view of London's
Barbican by Leah Yang.

above
A page from one of Alan
E. Cober's 'Cape Cod'
sketchbooks.

right
Studies by Manuel Marsol
for a 2022 exhibition and
Risograph-printed fanzine
inspired by Peter Weir's
film *Picnic at Hanging
Rock* (1975).

opposite
A page from one of Brian
Wildsmith's sketchbooks
showing early drafts
of his illustrations for
a 1990 edition of *The
Snow Country Prince*
by Daisaku Ikeda.

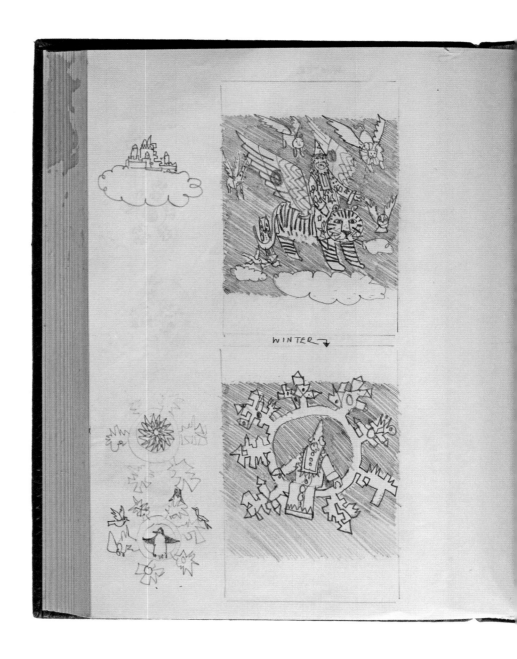

In the relatively short time since completing her education, Charlotte Ager has seen her reputation as an artist grow substantially, receiving numerous commissions from such newspapers and publishers as *The Guardian*, the *New York Times*, Penguin Random House and HarperCollins. Ager studied illustration

and animation at Kingston University before later completing the Drawing Year postgraduate programme at the Royal Drawing School in London.

'Sketchbooks for me are a place for playing, recording and reflecting. When I first used

them, like many I tried to make each spread something perfect until I learnt how valuable it was to have a space that wasn't that. I allow myself to make quick drawings – I can so easily turn the page and start again. This space allows me to learn quickly in a way I can't when at home in front of a page,

where I feel too precious and don't want to be wasteful. A sketchbook takes this pressure away; it's a space to build confidence.

'When I'm drawing, especially in a location or from life, often it feels like something is unlocked. I can just let my hands be consumed by moving a pencil around and my brain starts to feel more free. Or maybe it's actually more focused? I start drawing something and new images appear in my mind; I can finish that page and jump to the next one, shift the perspective, change the colours. I like using sketchbooks to return to places and keep looking again and again. Often, a first drawing is hesitant or a copy of something I've done before, but if I stick with it things start to appear I couldn't imagine when I started ... It's like magic.

'Quite rarely are the images in my sketchbooks directly lifted for commissioned works, but they play a vital part in the process nonetheless. They constantly provoke ways of seeing things that give my client work fresh insight. I often find new colour combinations in my sketchbooks because I tend to work quickly. The process feels more intuitive, and I come up with combinations that would feel too laboured in my studio at home. I also think sketchbooks are important as a way to reflect everyday life: you find yourself observing people and place more, and that seeps into your work. This means your practice remains connected to the world in some way, which feels important to me as an illustrator wanting my work to always feel accessible.

'My sketchbooks are also a stand-in for my memory, which is often very poor. I can remember exactly the feelings I had in a place just through a few recorded lines more than through photographs, because often

our idea of the world is elevated by our own experience and imagination. I often find I've curated moments of narrative in my sketchbooks. I've simultaneously pulled on observation and imagination to reflect the way my brain is processing a space, trying to find a sense of story. Sketchbooks have become a companion for me. Much like the way you experience and reminisce with friends or family, sketchbooks can reflect memories back at you and remind you of things you'd forgotten, cementing your place in the world.'

opposite, above & pages 12–15
The use of sketchbooks is vital to Charlotte Ager, allowing her to retain a sense of freshness and play in her work. They also provide her with a place to experiment with ways of translating complex subjects into subjective, instinctive responses.

Charlotte Ager

Illustrators' Sketchbooks

Charlotte Ager

Beatrice Alemagna

Over the last decade or so, the magical visual world of Beatrice Alemagna has finally found its way into the realm of English-language children's books. At the same time, her profound influence on the art of picturebook-making has become increasingly apparent, not least in the large number of accolades, awards and solo exhibitions that have come her way. It is also fair to say that the power of her work has played a significant role in breaking down barriers and creating opportunities for other artists whose highly personal, poetic and expressive art would, in the past, have likely been met with considerable caution by mainstream British and American publishers.

In 2022, at the 59th Bologna Children's Book Fair (BCBF), Alemagna was presented with an award created especially for her, one described by the organizers as an 'extraordinary award for an extraordinary artist'. The official announcement read: 'Like BCBF ... Beatrice Alemagna was born in Bologna, but she has gone on to become a true citizen of the world and one of the most esteemed illustrators on the international scene. With her latest work, the book *Vi går till parken* (Let's Go to the Park), published by the Swedish publisher Mirando Bok and written by Sara Stridsberg, she offers stunning proof of how art can represent a period of global crisis, such as the prolonged pandemic emergency, through a style that is both poetic and enlightening, without any trace of bombast.'

As a student in Urbino, Italy, Alemagna studied graphic design and typography, rather than formal drawing and painting, and it is only in recent years that she has begun to combine direct observation with purely imaginative drawing in her sketchbooks. Her visual vocabulary has been shaped primarily by her rich imagination and a sophisticated knowledge of art history.

'Sketches are an enormous part of the pleasure and freedom in my work. I see it as a necessary moment of playing. Sketching is to watch thoughts coming out of a pencil, to make anything I want, to rediscover some childhood feelings, to create strange shapes and to lose myself in a forest of unknown lines. They are an important part of inspiration for my own books. When I'm stuck or feel barren (in a creative drought), it's a primordial moment to reconnect myself with something lively and vibrant.'

opposite & pages 18–19
The sketchbooks of Beatrice Alemagna teem with drawings of people, animals, objects, buildings and movingly tender moments of human interaction, all rendered in soft pencil.

Beatrice Alemagna

Illustrators' Sketchbooks

Takako Aoki

left
A seasonal spread that reverses the usual relationship between green and white, using negative space to describe the tree.

opposite & pages 22–23
The theme of peace dominates these spreads from one of Takako Aoki's sketchbooks.

Born in Aomori, Japan, Takako Aoki studied design and oil painting in Tokyo. Her interest in illustration was given a boost when she twice entered a children's book illustration competition sponsored by Nissan and received prizes on both occasions. Her first picturebook soon followed, and she began to gain regular work as an illustrator, eventually relocating to Spain. As is the case for many young illustrators today, a large number of Aoki's commissions and sales come from her popular social-media accounts.

Aoki's sketchbooks are at the heart of her visual language. They are a place for instinctive, child-like graphic play, unselfconscious in their exuberance, incorporating collage,

paint, shape, texture and line, and delighting in the sheer joy of mark-making and design. Such features as block-printed type interact with both pictorial and abstract elements, contrasting rich colours with the negative space of the page. Animals feature throughout, in a compelling mix of the naive and the sophisticated, with pattern and design always at the forefront.

'The pictures in my sketchbooks are quite random. Usually, I haven't decided on a particular theme, and I haven't decided when to draw. But for me, drawing is like eating. After I have been drawing digitally, I need to draw by hand, using physical painting materials. I enjoy the texture of

painting materials and paper. It's like eating vegetables after eating meat, or wanting to eat sweets just after eating salty foods. I don't decide consciously which painting materials to use. My heart always chooses. The theme of what to draw just comes from the depths of my soul. I like nature and this planet. For me, drawing is healing, joy, nourishment and living.'

Peace :)

Takako Aoki

Peace :)

forvou

aje acababa
a por otros
como las
s madres.
nino de-
a recorda-
identidad;
o porque
e mo-
te hu-
rior de un
cuerdos de
ría. Lo poco

Illustrators' Sketchbooks

Takako Aoki

The sketchbooks of this consummate twentieth-century illustrator are legendary. They could perhaps be best described as 'visually garrulous'. Yet the dividing line between Ardizzone's sketchbooks and his finished illustrations is often barely discernible, so apparently free-flowing is the drawing in his multitude of published illustrations for books, magazines and advertising material that span some six decades. Within the carefully dated and numbered sketchbooks – many of which are held in the collection of the Ashmolean Museum in Oxford – can be found the very foundations for the visual language of their author, a language that became so familiar to generations of children and adults through much of the twentieth century.

Ardizzone drew directly from life only occasionally. Most of his drawings were made from immediate memory, whether he was still present at the location of the subject matter or had left it all together. The utterly narrative, anecdotal nature of his work is apparent in the little conversations, glances and gestures between the characters that populate the pages. Often, these form themselves into illustrated journals, handwritten text and image coming together on the page in the form of illustrated diaries of trips and events, such as a bibulous outing to Dieppe with fellow illustrator Barnett Freedman and Ardizzone's strikingly tall solicitor brother, David. This was published in full in Oliver Simon's graphic-arts journal, *Signature*. In the same year, 1951, *A Diary of a Holiday Afloat* – a similarly comedic sequence based on real events, this time with his family, doing battle with the elements on a riverboat on the Thames – was published in full in that year's edition of the annual *Saturday Book*.

In November 1952, Ardizzone was one of four people invited by the United Nations Educational, Scientific and Cultural Organization (UNESCO) to teach illustration and printmaking in India for six months. India and Ardizzone proved a perfect match, and, once again, he kept copious illustrated diaries of his experiences. These were eventually published in 1984 as *Indian Diary: 1952-53* by the Bodley Head, with an introduction by Malcolm Muggeridge. Bearing in mind that no other record of the trip was kept by UNESCO, Ardizzone's sketchbook drawings and written notes form an especially valuable historical record.

Just over a decade earlier, Ardizzone had employed his visual and textual sketchbook diaries to document and narrate less frivolous events during his time as an official war artist under Sir Kenneth Clark's ambitious scheme. Serving as a 2nd lieutenant, Ardizzone was in an anti-aircraft battery on Clapham Common in London when he received the news that he was to be sent to France to begin his new duties. His early experiences across the Channel, before the retreat from Dunkirk, were published by John Murray as *Baggage to the Enemy* (1941), an account in words and pictures of the comedies and tragedies of everyday lives affected by the war. Later, Ardizzone would travel through Sicily and join the Italian campaign. His working method consisted of making very quick visual and written notes on the spot in small sketchbooks before working up more developed drawings and watercolours back at base, wherever he could set up a table. Although Ardizzone's war drawings rarely show the horrors of combat, his deeply human record of its impact on the lives of those struggling to cope with what was going on around them is of unique importance.

opposite
Edward Ardizzone would occasionally use colour in his sketchbooks, as in this holiday study of bathers from 'Sketchbook 26'.

pages 26–27
Two spreads from 'Sketchbook 46'. In 1944, during his time as an official war artist, Ardizzone was, to his annoyance, kept in Portsmouth for a time, rather than being allowed to follow the Normandy landings. The Navy was sensitive about the artists' safety after the death of Eric Ravilious. In a letter to Edward Bawden, Ardizzone wrote, 'My best subjects were the WRNS [Women's Royal Navy Service]. They are enchanting.'

30th May Tuesday   Hervnel? . I escorted round
the Naval dockyards by Kennedy in the
morning. Enormous amount of material, and
lovely too but not
for me I'm afraid.
At least I can't
see anything there yet.
    Afternoon in my
room.

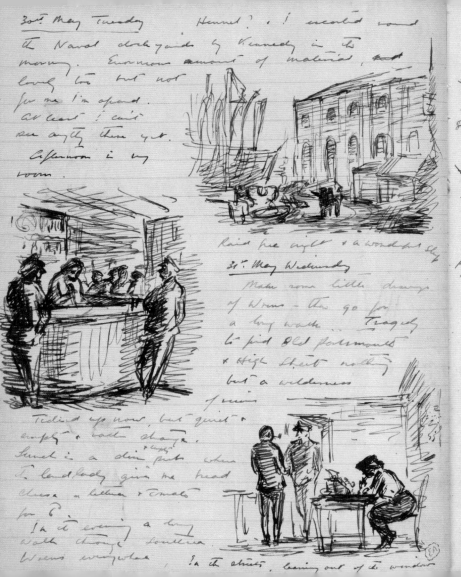

Raid free night + a wonderful sky

31st May Wednesday
        Make some little drawings
of Wrens - then go for
a long walk. Tragedy
to find Old Portsmouth
+ High Street nothing
but a wilderness
of ruins

Tidied up now, but quiet +
empty + rather strange.
Lunch in a dim pub where
the landlady gives me head
cheese, a lettuce + tomato
for 6.
    In the evening a long
walk through Southsea
Wrens everywhere   In the streets, leaning out of the windows

of the gay white houses on the
parade through which one could
see their double tiered bunks, or lounging in the front garden.

4

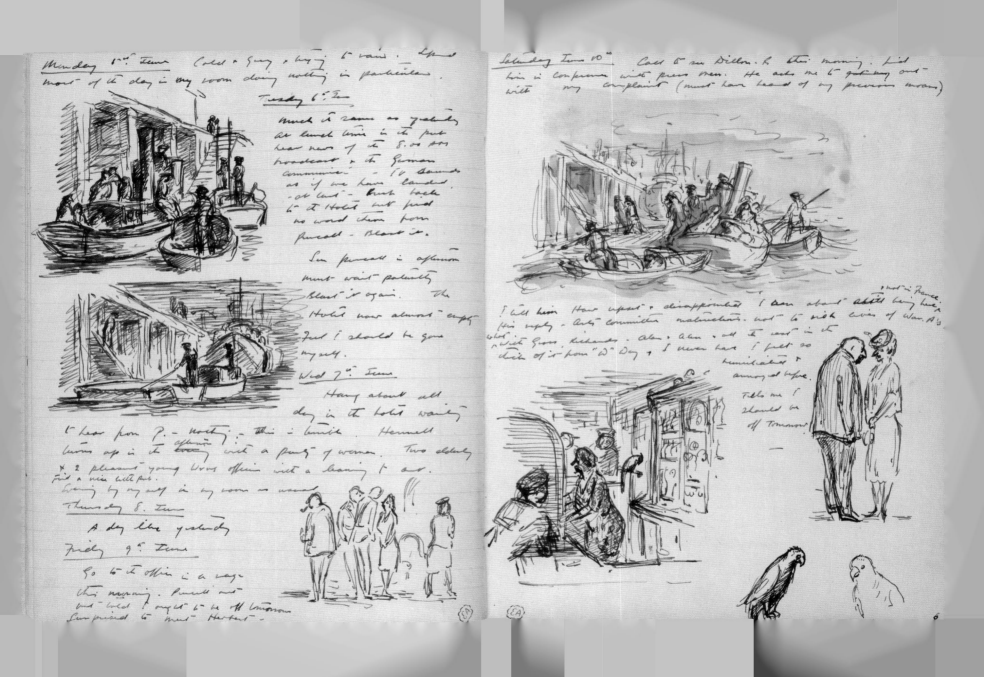

Monday 5th June — Cold & grey & beginning to rain. Spend most of the day in my room doing nothing in particular.

Tuesday 6th June

Much the same as yesterday. At lunch time in the pub hear news of the 8.00 a.m. broadcast & the German communiqué — It sounds as if we have landed — at least — rush back to the Hotel but find no word there from Purcell — Blast it.

See Purcell in afternoon — must wait patiently Blast it again. The Hotel now almost empty Feel I should be gone myself.

Wed 7th June

Hang about all day in the hotel waiting to hear from P. — nothing — this is terrible. Hemmell turns up in the afternoon with a party of women. Two elderly & 2 pleasant young Wrens officers with a leaning to art. Had a nice little pint.

Evening by myself in my room as usual.

Thursday 8 June

A day like yesterday

Friday 9th June

Go to the office in a rage this morning. Purcell out and told I ought to be off tomorrow Supposed to meet Herbert —

Saturday June 10th — Call to see Dillon. to this morning. Find him in conference with press men. He asks me to getting out with my complaint (must have heard of my previous moans)

I tell him How upset & disappointed I am about still being here — not in France. His reply — Anti committee instructions. not to risk lives of War. A's who with Gross, Richards. Alan & Alen, all the rest in the think of it from "W" Day + I never have I felt so humiliated & annoyed before.

Tells me I should be off Tomorrow

Edward Bawden

It is perhaps true to say that Edward Bawden, who has become one of the most celebrated of the mid-century British artist-illustrators, was not a natural or fluent draughtsman or sketchbook-user. His always meticulously composed images, whether made through the medium of drawing, painting or printmaking, flowed primarily from the process of *design*.

In the 1920s, having graduated from Cambridge School of Art, Bawden gained a scholarship to study design at the Royal College of Art, at a time when the new principal, William Rothenstein, was looking to modernize and shake off what he saw as the shackles of the Arts and Crafts era. Rothenstein brought in Paul Nash to teach in the Design School, and Nash had a major influence on both Bawden and his friend Eric Ravilious; he also had an impact on Barnett Freedman and Enid Marx, both of whom were in the Painting School but nevertheless leaned heavily towards the area of design. In an article about the new possibilities opening up for art and design in the world of industry, Nash later referred to the four of them as 'an outbreak of talent', led, as he saw it, by the outstanding work of Edward McKnight Kauffer.

Bawden's highly linear drawings are devoid of indulgent or gestural mark-making. He was a user of scrapbooks more than sketchbooks, yet these are equally fascinating, filled as they are with a mixture of drawings, printed ephemera, proofs of his own published work, letters, postcards and Christmas cards. The images shown here are taken from the book *English as She Is Spoke*, published in an edition of only 200 copies in 1960 by the Lion and Unicorn Press at the Royal College of Art. The book takes Bawden's Portugal drawings and sets them retrospectively to Pedro Carolino's 1855 *English as She Is Spoke*, an intended Portuguese–English phrasebook that has become a classic of accidental comedy. The original ink line drawings were presumably reproduced as proofs, to which Bawden then added hand-rolled or sponged areas of colour, immaculately conceived, as always, and sparingly applied. The two original line drawings shown on page 32 retain some of Bawden's pencil notes on intended colours. It is unclear, however, whether the drawings were cut from a sketchbook or if Bawden produced them on separate, individual sheets.

opposite & pages 30–31
Edward Bawden's line drawings, made on location in Portugal, were reproduced in the book *English as She Is Spoke* (1960), with colour added. Each spread was given its own specific limited colour palette, applied with Bawden's characteristic focus on design rather than pure realism.

Edward Bawden

The original ink line drawings from Edward Bawden's trip to Portugal, annotated with colour notes, shown alongside the final printed versions with colour added.

Thomas Bewick's influence on the history of illustration is immeasurable. He took the art of wood engraving to a new level, expressing his own passion for the natural world through his drawings. These he engraved on blocks of dense boxwood, across the end-grain, allowing for a very fine line to be cut with a graver while the wood was durable enough to withstand long print runs, in which text and image were printed together. His fame stems primarily from two ambitious books: *A General History of Quadrupeds,* published in 1790; and *History of British Birds,* published in two volumes, the first, *Land Birds,* in 1797 and the second, *Water Birds,* in 1804. The acclaim and commercial success of the former had encouraged Bewick to embark on the latter.

The exquisite technical skill and level of detail in Bewick's engraved work can be seen at its best in his famous print *The Wild Bull at Chillingham,* a metal facsimile of which was set into a paving stone in his home city of Newcastle in the north-east of England to commemorate the 250th anniversary of his birth in 2003. Having emerged from a humble background and an early apprenticeship to a commercial engraver, Ralph Beilby of Newcastle, Bewick was regarded by some as 'a craftsman, not an artist' – prejudice that was deepened by the perception that he was not from the 'gentleman class'. Others, however, including the artist and critic John Ruskin, were effusive in their praise. There was certainly far more than mere skill to Bewick's engraving. His injection of visual, anecdotal humour into his works, especially notable in his numerous little tailpieces for *History of British Birds* (as well as his illustrations for an edition of Aesop's fables), elevated the books beyond the purely informational.

It would seem that Bewick's preparatory work was executed primarily on loose sheets of paper. In 2017, however, the re-emergence of what is thought to be the artist's only surviving sketchbook, and possibly the only sketchbook he used, caused great excitement. The sketchbook was spotted at the San Francisco Book Fair by Anthony Smithson, a dealer in rare books from South Shields, a town close to Newcastle. Produced during the 1790s, its pages contain a fascinating mix of tonal drawings for engravings, with subjects including birds (preparatory drawings for *History of British Birds*), sheep, horses, pigs, cattle and, strangely, a hyena, which the artist may have seen at Gilbert Pidcock's travelling menagerie in 1799. In addition, many of the drawings are accompanied by detailed annotations, including measurements of the domestic farm animals' limbs and, in true illustrator's sketchbook fashion, detailed listings of the artist's expenses incurred during his working travels between clients. In 2017, the sketchbook was published in facsimile form by Jarndyce Antiquarian Booksellers, in an edition of 200 with an introduction and explanatory text by the Bewick scholar Nigel Tattersfield.

below, opposite & pages 36–39
The cover and a selection of pages from Thomas Bewick's only known sketchbook.

Thomas Bewick

Thomas Bewick

It would be difficult to overstate Quentin Blake's contribution to the field of illustration, both through his own long and distinguished career as an illustrator and through his founding of the Quentin Blake Centre for Illustration in north London. Scheduled for completion in 2024, the centre will be the world's largest public arts space devoted to illustration.

Born in 1932 in Sidcup, Kent, Blake was seemingly aware from an early age that drawing was what he most wanted to do. In his mid-teens, while still at grammar school, he was already sending cartoons to magazines such as *Punch*, and it wasn't long before some of them began to be accepted for publication. He chose to study literature at university, rather than go to art school, and gained a place at Downing College, Cambridge. While at Downing, he would often take the short walk across Parker's Piece to attend life-drawing classes at the Cambridge School of Art. Later, in London, he took twice-weekly drawing classes at Chelsea School of Art, a course of action motivated largely by the fact that one of the teachers at the school was the illustrator Brian Robb. Robb's influence on Blake was profound, but not only through his classes; when Robb later accepted the role of head of illustration at the Royal College of Art, he invited Blake to contribute to the teaching there. Blake would later take over Robb's position when the latter retired.

Throughout his years as a student at Cambridge, Blake continued to contribute cartoons to magazines, including the university's student publication, *Granta*, for which he would also occasionally act as guest art editor. For a number of years, he worked solely as a cartoonist, contributing regular 'one-off' visual gags in black and white and occasional full-colour cover designs for *Punch*. But his love of literature made the gradual move into book illustration inevitable. His first illustrations for books appeared in 1960, in *Come Here Till I Tell You* (Hutchinson) by Patrick Campbell, whom he had met at *The Spectator* magazine, and *A Drink of Water and Other Stories* (Faber) by John Yeoman, an author he has since collaborated with on numerous projects.

Blake's instantly recognizable drawings are often described as 'spontaneous', but their animated nature is the result of careful planning. In order to keep control of the composition while still retaining movement and gesture, Blake uses a lightbox and works on thick paper, which allows just enough of the compositional shapes of the rough drawings to shine through but not enough to inhibit the freedom of the 'redraw'. His very earliest visual thoughts and compositional studies are often made in unassuming lined notebooks. The one shown here, for example, contains ideas that would eventually evolve into *Angelica Sprocket's Pockets*, published by Red Fox in 2011.

opposite & pages 42–43
Taken from a simple, lined exercise book, the pages shown here contain Quentin Blake's early workings for 'The Pocket Book', an idea that would eventually become *Angelica Sprocket's Pockets*. The drawings are in the form of the roughest of sketches, focusing primarily on page design, yet the characters are already very much 'alive'.

Herbert Pocket
pulls on his vest

Herbert Pocket
is getting dressed.

4.

His overcoat hangs
behind the door.

5.

His overcoat has pockets
galore.

His overcoat nearly reaches
the ground

The overcoat pockets go
all the
way round.

6.

7

Quentin Blake

Percy Drake Brookshaw

For most of the generation of male British artist-illustrators who trained at art school in the 1920s and 1930s, the Second World War would form a lengthy hiatus in their careers. Some, who had already established a level of status in the field, such as Edward Ardizzone, Edward Bawden and Leonard Rosoman, were fortunate enough to be appointed as official war artists via the scheme established by Sir Kenneth Clark. The scheme provided a level of protection from front-line action, although not enough to save Bawden's close friend Eric Ravilious, who perished when the military plane in which he was travelling went missing over the sea near Iceland in 1942.

Percy Drake Brookshaw (who usually signed his work 'Drake Brookshaw') was born in the London borough of Southwark in 1907. He trained at London's Central School of Arts and Crafts in the 1920s under John Farleigh, having been encouraged into the field of illustration by the great poster designer F. Gregory Brown. By the late 1930s, Brookshaw was building a successful career designing book covers, contributing illustrations to such publications as the *Radio Times*, and, notably, designing posters for London Underground. It was a boom time for poster design, particularly for London Underground, where the legendary Frank Pick was championing high-quality art and design for industry in his capacity as chief executive officer at the London Passenger Transport Board. Brookshaw was becoming particularly known for his poster designs featuring major sporting events, including the FA Cup final, the Wimbledon tennis championships and the annual Boat Race on the River Thames between Oxford and Cambridge universities.

When the war interrupted his artistic career, he initially trained as an air gunner. Like many artists, however, he was tasked with applying his skills to the design of camouflage, in his case at RAF Manston in Kent. Later, as Flying Officer Brookshaw, he worked as an interpreter of aerial photographs, an extremely important role in military terms.

Brookshaw's ink-and-wash observational sketchbook studies shown here were executed in 1944 during the Italian campaign, as the Allies moved north through the country. They provide an intimate glimpse into the world of the off-duty soldier in a way that photography could never do – the careful examination of the everyday paraphernalia of the soldier, the sense of exhaustion combined with temporary tranquillity. The drawings first came to light when they were displayed and sold by a well-known London fine-art gallery. Brookshaw would successfully resume his illustration career after the war, continuing to specialize in poster design into the 1960s, in particular for the growing holiday-camp market.

opposite
'Frank sitting on Veranda in the sun, 28th Jan, 44, San Severo'. Brookshaw and his team had reached San Severo, a town in the province of Foggia, Apulia, south-eastern Italy, after travelling up from Tunisia.

above
These careful studies of unpopulated interiors and the Italian light that spills into them provide an invaluable insight into the daily lives and 'downtime' of some of those involved in the Italian campaign.

right
A sepia ink-and-wash study with some pencil under-drawing, dated 25 April 1944.

Percy Drake Brookshaw

this page
A sense of the temporary respite from the horrors of war experienced by off-duty soldiers is perfectly conveyed in these studies of servicemen washing or writing letters home.

opposite
A fellow officer reads a two-month-old copy of a newspaper.

21st FEB 44 In billets Italy.
Jimmy reads 2 months
old Weekly "Mirror"

Percy Drake Brookshaw

Calef Brown

There is a raw, primitive, 'folksy' yet playful feel to the illustrative work of Calef Brown. Brown is an artist for whom there appears to be a seamless, freewheeling overlap among creative play, so-called personal work and published pieces, whether visual or textual. They are all tied together by a unifying sense of rhythm. This synthesis is perhaps also not entirely unconnected to the fact that Brown is a habitual sketchbook-user.

Brown's creations as a poet, illustrator, picturebook-maker and musician seem to flow into and through one another in an entirely natural way. A love of wordplay and nonsense has inevitably led him to illustrate not only his own poetry but also that of Edward Lear. Alongside the many books he has authored, Brown has worked widely in the field of advertising, for clients such as Adidas, Coca-Cola and Levi Strauss. He has also produced illustrations for some of the most well-known magazines in America, including *Rolling Stone*, *Time*, the *New Yorker*, *Travel & Leisure* and *Newsweek*.

Over the years, across many highly successful and award-winning books, Brown's work has evolved to become less figurative or representational and increasingly instinctive and pattern-led. He cites the book *Knust*, published in 2013 by the influential Norwegian publishing house Magikon, with text by Hege Siri, as a turning point in his work, along with his own book of two years later, *Hypnotize a Tiger* (Henry Holt). He says:

'They were the first things I'd done using a more graphic approach, which came out of my sketchbook work. For the first few years of my career, my sketchbooks were mainly utilitarian – for thumbnailing and sketches specifically related to editorial and other freelance jobs. Similarly, in the late 1990s, when I began writing and illustrating children's books, I would keep sketchbooks devoted to brainstorming, writing and composing images and spreads solely for that aspect of my practice. About ten years ago I began devoting some sketchbooks to more experimental use – drawing freely and improvising, mostly with brush and ink. I wanted to create a new voice, a more line-centric one that was different from my established shape-based, flat acrylic style. This way of working with brush and ink led directly to it being used in two published children's books, as well as sparking new processes for my personal work and some fun traditional–digital hybrid methods.'

For illustration students, sketchbooks are an important window into the thinking and processes behind the public-facing work of such successful artists as Brown. Currently an associate professor at Rhode Island School of Design in Providence, Brown has taught at Otis College of Art and Design, Los Angeles; Emily Carr University of Art + Design, Vancouver; and ArtCenter College of Design, Pasadena.

opposite & pages 50–51
The sketchbook pages of Calef Brown shown here are primarily a place for experimentation with shapes, colours and patterns, as well as the interplay between these and more figurative elements.

SNail's PaCE

Bankrupt sculptor.
Stuck in the RED.
HE NEEDED a hand
but forged a head.

Bankrupt
Sculptor
Stuck in the RED
HE NEEDED a hand
but forged a head.

a BANKRUPT sculptor.
stuck in THE RED.
HE NEEDED a hand
but forged a head.

The exquisite visual storytelling of Cai Gao transcends numerous boundaries and creates links between the many cultures that so often seem mutually exclusive. Her visual vocabulary was initially forged during the Cultural Revolution, when she found herself exiled and working as a schoolteacher deep in the Chinese countryside. It was against this backdrop of rural isolation from the late 1960s to the early 1980s that she immersed herself in her painting, as well as patchwork, inspired by a deep affection for the landscape. The bridges that Cai has managed to build with her art include those between traditionalism and modernism, between Eastern and Western visual culture, and between the fine and applied arts. The last of these are often regarded, especially in the West, as among the most difficult worlds to reconcile.

In a country where the children's picturebook has only recently begun to be recognized as a unique artform, Cai, over many decades, has brought a rare combination of technical skill and vision to her graphic storytelling, employing her exceptional draughtsmanship, painting skills and sumptuous use of colour in the service of the modern picturebook. Although she might rightly be seen in many respects as a pioneer, the key qualities that underpin her work are both deeply personal and universal: a love of nature and a very human vision. Perhaps this explains the burgeoning cross-cultural appeal of her output.

As Cai explains, her sketchbooks form an integral part of her identity as an artist:

'I like to write and draw at the same time, probably because of my picturebook habit. I make sketches to keep track of my mind.

Rather like making patchwork, I "sew" my daily observations into my sketchbook, stroke by stroke. I like handwork. Life becomes warm and loving because of handwork.

'My sketching is actually a form of talking to myself, visually. While taking notes can clear my mind and help me figure things out, drawing can do something else: dealing with feelings and emotions that are beyond words. A lot of things come into my sketchbook, uninvited. But somehow I feel I had been waiting for them for a long time.

'My sketchbooks are like a mirror: they mirror the sky, light, cloud, shadow ... almost everything in my life. With words, the mirror is much clearer.

'Plants grow every day and so do children. It would be a shame if I didn't pay attention to them. I discover many interesting things that I can't afford to forget. So I draw them, quickly. I enjoy collecting interesting things and ideas in everyday life, but how can I preserve them? A camera can't do it well, nor a computer. Only sketchbooks. They are like storage bins, or cabinets for keeping things fresh, keeping my collection safe and alive.

'Wherever I go, my sketchbook comes with me. I like sketchbooks of different sizes and textures for recording different things. Words are also treated as visual elements and are part of the composition. If I go somewhere in the country for a few weeks, my sketchbooks fill up especially quickly.'

opposite & pages 54–55
Cai Gao's intense feelings for the beauty to be found in everyday things are apparent in her much-used notebooks, in which she seeks to capture experiences of places and people before they escape.

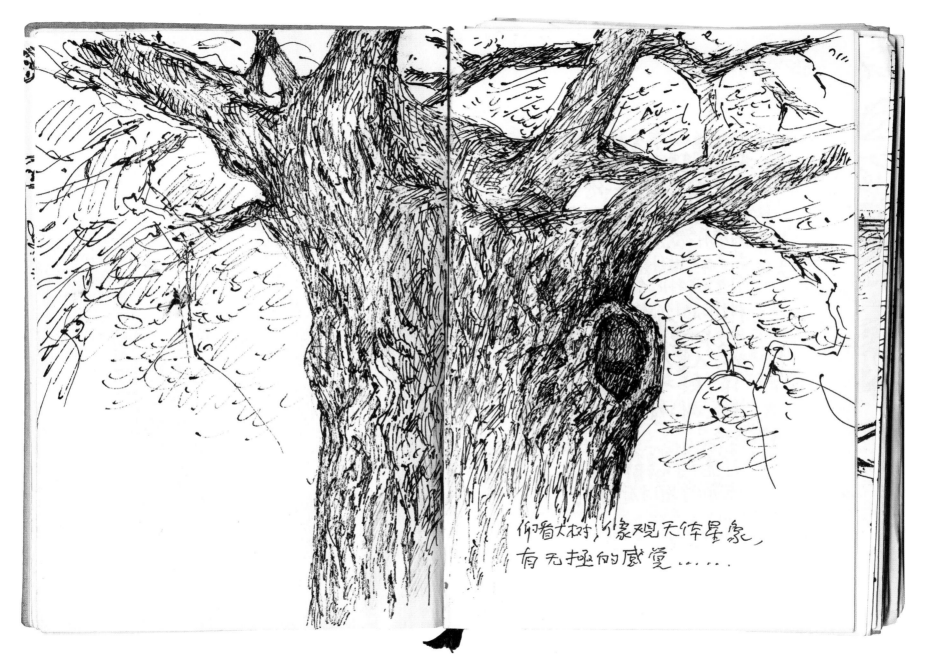

仰看大树，好象观天体星象，
有无极的感觉……

Cai Gao

哪是一颗什么样子呢？橡皮筋吗，它们爬到一米的高度又川变着它的杉木把回去了。杉木这么粗，大约要长廿+年吧，它的枝条长着长着也是朝下垂着的

这五个人扎在
这一堆很好玩的样子，你知道他们在干吗，
他们都在看浅水池里几尾鱼，
并往池子里那着个石子！人在鱼面前的的举动
实的是太让人难为情了。

早晨来得很早，五点钟天就大亮了。六点钟左右，有引擎发动的声音和摩托车驰过的声音。摩托车上基本上都是一男载一女，那是男人们送女人到大大小小的客栈打工的人。他们把车停下来，一个个睡眼醒松，瞇睡没醒的男人掏出手机拨弄，好像忙不赢的样子。女人则站在坪里梳头发，梳成一个髻，然后提着桶去上班，看样子清洁工是上班最早的人。

第二早的算厨房师傅，一个喜欢做手撕鱼炒青辣椒拌竹吃的人。但是手总是有小动作，二馈说，何解我们也给辣椒鱼只有鱼皮冒得鱼肉喽？ 女也开始研究，研究
结果是，鱼肉都码到搞厨房里
的人手端的石碗里去了。"她们
碗里手撕鱼一它它的，尽是肉，
冒得皮的"，她报告说。"她
的眼睛就尖来！"

衣服的人。
特喜欢军格子
大厨，一个
老调

"旅游宾馆最塑，态度塑，饭菜
塑，他们的员工都说，不要介绍旅
游宾馆……" 杨教授爱党的

男人
女人
员工甲
员工乙

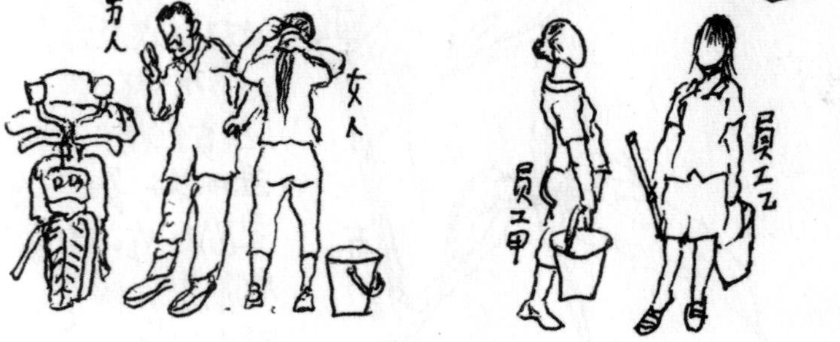

Having studied illustration as an undergraduate and then specialized in children's book illustration at postgraduate level, Emma Carlisle found success in the latter discipline relatively quickly. In 2013, while still a student, she had entered the Macmillan Prize for Children's Book Illustration and been highly commended; her first book, *Lion Practice*, was then taken up by the same publisher and issued in 2015. A second self-authored picturebook, *Bears on the Beach*, was released the following year. *Lion Practice* has subsequently been nominated for various publishing awards, including the Kate Greenaway Medal and the Klaus Flugge Prize.

Perhaps more than any other artist featured in this book, Carlisle has always been acutely aware of the differences she perceived between her sketchbooks and her more public-facing work, in terms of both personal satisfaction and her emotional relationship to each. In 2018, in the interests of her health, she took the decision to step back from her undergraduate teaching work and take time out to focus on landscape painting, which had long been a key interest. Four years later, while continuing to paint, Carlisle returned to picturebook-making with *What Do You See When You Look at a Tree?*, published by Big Picture Press and the Royal Botanic Gardens, Kew. It is a book that clearly comes from the heart as well as from her beloved sketchbooks, incorporating and informed by the painting skills that have arguably given greater depth and confidence to her work.

'My best work has always been in sketchbooks. At university, this felt frustrating because I struggled to create final artwork, and my feedback was often the same: "there is better work in your sketchbooks". After graduating, I tried not using sketchbooks and worked on loose sheets of paper, but the problem was still the same. There is a safety to sketchbooks that you don't get anywhere else. They feel like a home for your drawings. If something doesn't quite work, you can turn the page and start again or shut the book and walk away. I now use sketchbooks almost exclusively. From ideas to experiments with materials, even the final artwork for my latest picturebooks was created in sketchbooks.

'I'm often working in two (or more) sketchbooks at the same time. Whether I'm life-drawing, out on the coast path or experimenting in the studio, I find drawing in multiple sketchbooks lets me flit between several drawings or ideas at once.

'For a while, I tried to separate my projects into different sketchbooks. I had a sketchbook for location drawing, a sketchbook for animals, and a sketchbook for life-drawing, etc. Now I put everything together, which means I've been able to make connections between different areas of my work. Having all my drawings jumbled together makes them feel like a visual diary, and I can see myself working things out like a puzzle, which is visually and mentally enjoyable!'

opposite & pages 58–61
This selection of spreads from Emma Carlisle's sketchbooks, which includes life-drawings and landscapes of Devon and Cornwall, clearly reveals the internal dialogue between painter and illustrator.

Illustrators' Sketchbooks

Emma Carlisle

Chloë Cheese

Chloë Cheese spent her childhood in the now famous 'artists' village' of Great Bardfield in rural Essex, surrounded by many of the British artist-illustrators whose work has become so celebrated in recent years. Edward and Charlotte Bawden were living in Brick House along the road, originally shared with Eric and Tirzah Ravilious, while Walter Hoyle, John Aldridge and Michael Rothenstein were a short walk away as well. Chloë's parents, Sheila Robinson and Bernard Cheese, were both artist-printmakers who also worked in the field of commercial illustration, and it seemed entirely natural that Chloë should follow suit.

In 1972, after studying briefly at Cambridge School of Art, Chloë gained a place at the Royal College of Art (RCA) in London and spent a period of time working at the college's studios in Paris. Speaking to Ian Massey in 2002 about her experience as a student, she said: 'The notion of the artist/illustrator was very familiar to me, and I always intended to follow in the footsteps of the previous generation. At art school I was quite surprised to find that this had become an almost anachronistic ambition, but I found, and still do, that it suited my interest very well.' Indeed, within a very short time after leaving the RCA, Chloë and her work had become

widely known in both disciplines, with solo exhibitions in leading galleries in London and Osaka alongside illustration commissions from such leading publications and design groups as the *Sunday Times*, *The Observer* and Habitat. Book commissions flooded in too, for cover designs, interior illustrations (especially those dealing with culinary topics) and full picturebooks. She now concentrates primarily on printmaking.

The sketchbook has been central to the development of Chloë's highly distinctive visual language. Her drawn line, as with her handwriting, flows naturally, appearing to be in continuous contact with the surface of the paper as it travels around, with just occasional variations in pressure and emphasis.

'At sixteen, I was a diligent art student at Cambridge Art School drawing in my sketchbook every day, which helped in building an ease with drawing and observation. My mother always stressed the importance of drawing and had some fascinating sketchbooks of her own from student days. Now I use my sketchbooks less frequently and usually as a resource for printmaking. I find that, in my drawings, I am grasping the core of what interests me by observing over a period of time, say

one or two hours. Photographs taken as reference cannot do this as they contain too much extraneous information. My drawings of buildings and places are defined by the passers-by who are very much of my time and moment. An artist whose work I admire, Anthony Gross, had the same interest in the anonymous passer-by. Spending years as an illustrator has meant that I have constantly been drawing and exploring the narrative possibilities that arise from the process. That my style of drawing has changed over the decades is evident in my sketchbooks, which are the most direct and personal example of anyone's work.

'I keep all my sketchbooks as they are always useful but partly too for sentimental reasons. I tend to regret selling a page as each page feels important and personal. I still remember, slightly regretfully, selling a Paris sketchbook page to Quentin Blake when I was a student.

'At the moment, I use a Moleskine sketchbook, which contains lovely smooth, off-white paper, and a soft pencil kept sharp to draw with.'

opposite
A spread from one of Chlöe Cheese's Venice sketchbooks.

pages 64–65
Drawings of London Zoo, Crystal Palace Park, Pollock's Toy Museum and two further sketches of Venice, all alive with anecdotal detail.

pages 66–67
Two examples of Chlöe Cheese's sketchbooks from her days as a student at London's Royal College of Art. Her flair for composition and typical flattening of perspective were already in evidence.

Bridge Fondamenta
S. Misericordia

Chloë Cheese

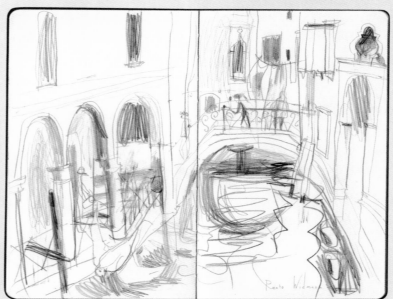

Illustrators' Sketchbooks

A selfie on
blue hair early the bridge
evening Misericordia

red.

Chloë Cheese

Sunkyung Cho

Although Sunkyung Cho and his insatiable creative and intellectual appetite may not be familiar to many in the West, he is something of a hero to the numerous leading book-makers who have been fortunate enough to be invited to his picturebook school in his native South Korea. Born in Seoul in 1959, Cho grew up in a family torn apart by war. He studied graphic design and illustration at the esteemed Hongik University in his home city, then moved to New York to study at the School of Visual Arts on the MFA Illustration as Visual Essay programme founded by the late but legendary Marshall Arisman. After graduation, his work began to appear in such publications as the *New York Times*.

In addition to being a painter, illustrator and picturebook-maker, Cho has also turned his hand to film-set design. His deeply personal picturebooks include *Underground Garden* (2008), published in six languages, and *Blue Bird* (2009), which explores a mother's ultimate sacrifice of 'letting go' of her child in a manner that embodies Cho's passionate belief that picturebooks can be for adults as well as for children. This conviction is also at the heart of his teaching. Among the illustrators and academics who have travelled to Seoul to give lectures at the Some Picturebook Institute, founded by Cho in 2003, are his old tutor Arisman, Beatrice Alemagna, Chloé Poizat, Katsumi Komagata, Valerio Vidali and Chris Haughton.

Haughton has written about his friendship with Cho and the debt he feels he owes him, not only for allowing him to sleep on his studio couch for five months, but also for sharing his thoughts on picturebooks; at the time, Cho was working on *Blue Bird* while Haughton was putting together his debut picturebook, *A Bit Lost* (2010). Although very different in approach, both books share similar underlying messages. *A Bit Lost* would go on to be one of the most successful debut picturebooks, translated into nineteen languages and launching its creator's huge international profile.

In yet another aspect to his work, Cho's small independent publishing company, Some Books, publishes limited editions of innovative picturebooks and artists' books, often created by his own graduates and often handbound at the Some Institute workshops. Many of these have been purchased by leading international museums and cultural institutions.

Cho has kept a daily illustrated diary/notebook for the last twenty years, religiously laying down his thoughts in both words and pictures. Such thoughts can be random musings, quotes or visual ideas, sometimes sequential, sometimes stand-alone.

'Over the last two decades, my diary has become a sketchbook. It is "writing with pictures" mostly. Of course, I do write with words too, but I start thinking with images and later add words if necessary. Even before I start consciously thinking, my drawing starts without any concept or plan. Generally, this process is not just for drawing in the diary but for my painting too. Thinking with images is my process in art. I believe that somewhere within me, the image has formed and is waiting to speak out. This form is not an abstract concept, it is a physical form like my body.'

opposite & pages 70–71
The daily drawings and notes made by Sunkyung Cho reveal the constant creative enquiry and reflection that drives this artist and teacher. Cho's artwork can often be dark and disturbing, especially when contrasted with Antoine de Saint-Exupéry's Little Prince on the cover of a 2021 diary (opposite, top right).

FRIDAY
January
15

✴ big hand! big dream!

SATURDAY
January
16

"100"
✴ most important things in the world.

78. BLACK COTTON SWAB.

✴ "100" most important things for the little prince

4. red(ish) fox.
because of the little prince learn
about tames from fox which is
"One only understands the things that one tames"
said the fox. men have no more time to understand
anything. they buy things all ready made at the shops
but there is no shops anywhere where one can buy
friendship so men have no friend anymore. "If
you want a friend tame me" "What must I do
to tame you? asks the little prince. "You must
be very patient." replied the fox. "first you
will sit down at a little distance from me —
like that — in the grass, I shall look at you
out of the corner of my eye, and you will
say nothing. words are the source of mis-
understanding ..."

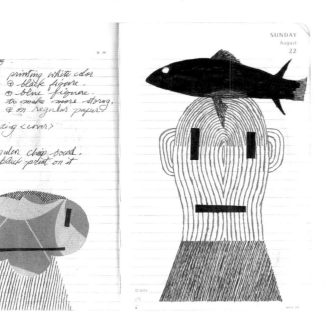

SATURDAY
August
21

✴ inside printing
printing white color
⊕ black figure.
⊕ blue figure.
to make more strong.
⊕ on regular paper.

✴ out side printing ⟨cover⟩
regular cheap board.
⊕ black print on it

✴

SUNDAY
August
22

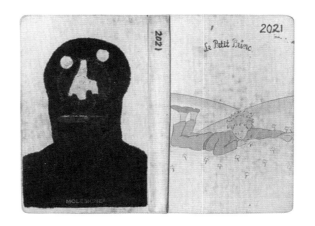

2021
2021
Le Petit Prince
MOLESKINE

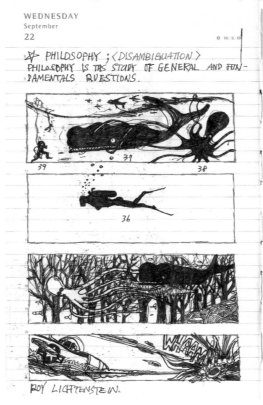

WEDNESDAY
September
22

✴ PHILOSOPHY ; ⟨DISAMBIGUATION⟩
PHILOSOPHY IS THE STUDY OF GENERAL AND FUN-
DAMENTALS QUESTIONS.

ROY LICHTENSTEIN.

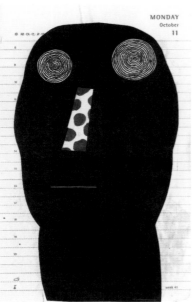

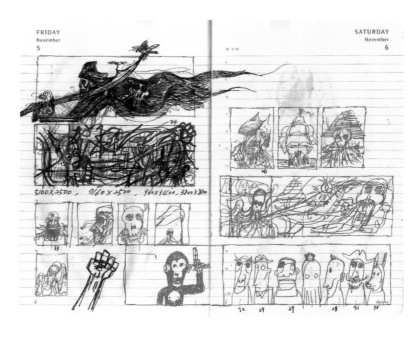

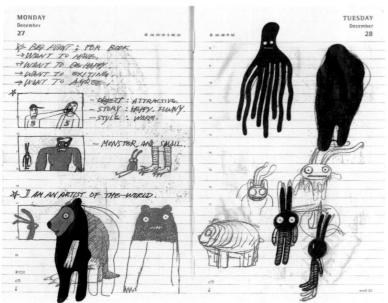

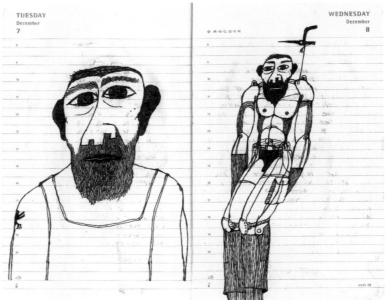

Illustrators' Sketchbooks

Alan E. Cober

Born in 1935 in the Bronx, New York City, Alan E. Cober was a pioneer of visual journalism. He was never afraid to approach an art director or magazine editor with a portfolio of highly personal drawings that examined in a focused and individual way a particular subject or issue and suggest that it be published as a visual essay. His father was a criminal lawyer, and Cober soon developed a fascination for courtrooms, the legal process and the rights of the underprivileged. He would often accompany his father on visits to his clients, incarcerated in the Manhattan jail known as 'The Tombs' (now the Manhattan Detention Complex). In her introduction to the 2012 Dover edition of *The Forgotten Society*, a collection of her father's drawings subtitled *Lives Out of Sight in Nursing Homes, Prisons, and Mental Institutions*, Leslie Cober-Gentry recalls how childhood holidays would often take the family to places connected to her father's work, where he would combine family life with research for ongoing projects:

'Long walks on the beach were an excuse to find interesting objects to draw in his sketchbook, whether it was part of a crab shell, which he would turn into a drawing in his sketchbook titled "Conversation for One", or a decaying dead bird that he would collect and sit down and draw. Cober was compulsive about drawing from nature and capturing both its grit and beauty in his sketchbooks. He was a fanatic about keeping journals – hundreds of them ... He had hundreds of sketchbooks stored across the shelves of his studio, each one filled with adventures, vacations, people, and animals from different parts of the world.'

The urgency with which Cober worked, his evident need to 'capture the moment' before it escaped, meant that he often combined written notes with drawings, his spidery handwriting merging seamlessly with the drawn line.

One of Cober's high-profile reportage projects came about when, in 1987, he called the then art director of *Rolling Stone* magazine, Fred Woodward, with the idea of following Pope John Paul II around during his visit to the United States, sketchbook in hand. His daughter recalls turning on the television news at the time and seeing her father standing just a few feet from the Pope, drawing in his sketchbook.

Over the course of a career full of fearless and incisive graphic commentary, Cober was commissioned not only by *Rolling Stone* but also by the likes of *Esquire*, *The Atlantic*, *Life* magazine and the *New York Times*. He received numerous national and international awards and his work is now held in multiple permanent collections and museums. Cober also taught at the University at Buffalo, New York, as a distinguished visiting artist until his death in 1998.

right & opposite
Pages from Alan E. Cober's 1980 'presidential sketchbook', with personal messages from the then US president, Jimmy Carter, and his successor, Ronald Reagan.

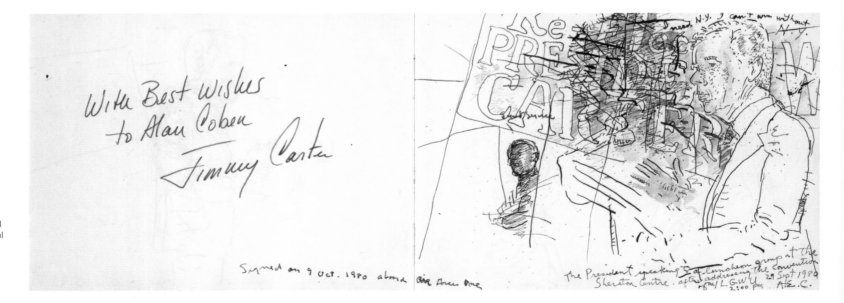

Brown
Suit

Brown
tie

Ronald Reagan
10/2/80

"Small" business *unclear* *unclear*
Gov. Reagan signed the drawing between - Pittsburgh & GreenBay. at the Waldorf Astoria - 9:50 AM
1 Oct 1980 Alan E. Cober

Alan E. Cober

above & opposite
Pages from Cober's
'Cape Cod' sketchbooks.

6 Sept 86 -

Alan E. Cober

Columbia, South Carolina St. Peter's church 12 Sept 19·87   A E C

above & opposite
Two pages from the
sketchbook used by Cober
for the *Rolling Stone*
commission to document
Pope John Paul II's visit to
the United States.

SAN ANTONIO. TEXAS. 11:43. 13 Sept 87
Temp - 90 degrees. The Pope the Lords day Sunday
which he does better than English.
Of course I don't understand Spanish - but then again
she didn't get any applause.
People are passing out

Alan E. Cober

Christopher Corr

Christopher Corr has worked for more than forty years across a wide range of disciplines, including book illustration, advertising, editorial and stamp design, winning numerous awards along the way. In addition to his commissioned illustration work, he has exhibited in numerous solo and group exhibitions. Corr's output is instantly recognizable for its expressive, fearless and playful use of colour – childlike yet highly sophisticated. For him, the sketchbook, commissioned illustration and gallery painting are inextricably linked. His work draws on his extensive travels with a sketchbook to North Africa, the United States and, perhaps most importantly, India, whose colours and traditions find their way into much of his imagery.

Corr studied graphic design and illustration first at Manchester Polytechnic (now Manchester Metropolitan University) and then at the Royal College of Art in London, where his supervisor for his master's was Quentin Blake, the then head of illustration. Like so many who received a traditional art-school education, Corr describes his foundation course as 'just the most incredible experience ... being able to draw and paint and print and take photos all day long'.

Corr's travels, his experience of other cultures and the sketchbooks that have accompanied him have played a significant role in shaping the multicultural and inclusive nature of his work. Unsurprisingly, Corr has cited Miroslav Šašek and his 'This is ...' illustrated travel books as a key influence. As with Šašek, the ways in which other people live their lives seems to be a recurring theme in Corr's work, whether self-generated or commissioned, and a significant number of his book-illustration commissions have been in the field of folk tales and traditions from around the world.

His richly sensuous paintings, sometimes described as naive, are constructed in a flat, schematic idiom and teem with all human (and often animal) life. A tangible sense of celebration and empathy flows through them all. Generally, they are painted in gouache on carefully chosen handmade papers, from India or Italy.

The travel sketchbooks, as well as being filled with richly evocative, painterly and intuitive responses to place, are often full of indigenous graphic ephemera – bus tickets, advertising flyers, packaging and so on. Corr frequently refers back to these sketchbooks when working on his picturebooks. This was especially true in the case of *The Great Race: The Story of the Chinese Zodiac* (Lincoln Children's Books, 2019), for which he returned to studies made in the Li River valley, Guilin, China, many years previously.

'I have always kept sketchbooks ... I carry a big sketchbook and a small one with me and a few black ink pens to draw with, a bulldog clip, a small box of watercolours and a few brushes and some water. I would feel lost without my kit. I use a lot of different sketchbooks, some to paint in and others to draw in. I have scrapbooks to keep the interesting ephemera that I find. I try not to mix up my books ...

'When I was a student in Manchester, I worked in sketchbooks most of the time, and I used them to get to know the city. I went out most days to draw and record new places, and in a short time I became familiar with the city ... Later, while I was at the Royal College of Art, I won a Leverhulme scholarship to travel and draw in the USA. I spent five months travelling across the country, drawing everything I saw ... I wanted to record huge skyscrapers in the big cities and to see the buildings of émigré architects from Europe. For a long time I had seen and admired Paul Hogarth's drawings of the US, busy cityscapes with big cars and gigantic buildings. He always used a small sketchbook to map out his drawings before committing to a large final piece. It was a useful tip. You must ensure that your drawing fits on the paper, even in your sketchbooks.

'I use my sketchbooks to experiment and to make discoveries ... I like to buy sketchbooks in the places where I travel to and to draw in them during my journey. In China I found extremely long concertina books, ideal for wide panoramas, and in India I bought books with handmade papers in cotton, rice or grass. In Rajasthan I bought a beautiful, red quilted book with lots of pages and a string to tie it closed. I noticed the alarm on some people's faces when I opened the book in public only to discover it was a debt collector's accounts book.

'In India I drew all the time and tried to record everything ... there was so much to take in. I learnt to draw walking down the street. Lately, in France, I have been painting on old Livre de Poche paperbacks. I really like working with the text and the paper. It adds something to the atmosphere of the piece I'm making.

'Sketchbooks are so personal to the creator ... I love to look at other artists' sketchbooks and to see their thought processes in action. The seascapes and sky studies of Turner are astonishing. Picasso's journals of drawings are so inspiring and exciting. The sketchbooks of William Kentridge come alive through animation and music.

'A sketchbook is a place to lose yourself, and to discover new worlds.'

A spread from one
of Christopher Corr's
Morocco sketchbooks:
'Pink mud walls, Essaouira'.

opposite left
The collaged, hand-painted cover of one of Christopher Corr's Venice sketchbooks.

opposite right
'Venice and Grand Canal', the opening image from a Venice sketchbook. Corr used a 'wet on wet' technique to heighten the watery effect.

right
Colour studies of a Moroccan hammam – the public baths and steam rooms that are a part of everyday life in the country – made on a locally printed book.

Christopher Corr

opposite
'Tibetan prayer wheels', painted on fragile, handmade paper with a considerable amount of show-through.

far left
'Mint tea in Marrakech'.

left
'Olive stalls in Barjac Market'.

below
'Aigues-Mortes and swallows', made during Christopher Corr's travels in the South of France.

Christopher Corr

Kenyon Cox saw his work as an illustrator primarily as a means of supporting his painting. During his lifetime, however, it was his illustration work for magazines and advertising for which he was perhaps more widely known. Cox was also an influential tutor at the Art Students League of New York, where he taught regularly during the institution's early years, and whose logo he designed. A devoted traditionalist, Cox was an advocate of the purest academic and realist approaches to drawing, at a time when, especially in his later years, more modern, avant-garde approaches to fine art were emerging from Europe.

Cox was born in Ohio in 1856, to a philanthropic family of theologians and politicians. He studied initially at the Art Academy of Cincinnati but soon moved to the Pennsylvania Academy of Fine Arts, which he believed would give him a better chance of realizing his dream of furthering his studies in Europe. He eventually moved to Paris in 1877, becoming a student in the atelier of the artist Carolus-Duran (Charles August Émile Durand). Cox, however, found his tutor's high-society portrait painting rather 'vulgar' and enrolled at the École des Beaux Arts, where he studied under the painter and sculptor Jean-Léon Gérôme. He remained in Europe – taking the opportunity to travel through France and Italy to broaden his artistic horizons and visit the more important Renaissance works – until 1882, when he returned to the United States.

Settling in New York, Cox found success as a muralist, his classical, allegorical approach featuring theatrical figures earning him commissions for a range of public buildings, including libraries and courtrooms. It was in New York that he produced much of his illustration work. He also became a respected art critic, regularly writing articles for such publications as the *New York Evening Post*, *Century* and *Scribner's Magazine*. His writing was often in the form of a fiercely mounted defence of traditional representation in art in the face of the invading 'modern styles'. His books have endured, featuring as they do deeply informed instruction and practical explanation around the underlying basics of image-making.

Cox's sketchbooks clearly demonstrate his draughtsmanship and deep attachment to classical approaches in painting and drawing.

left
Cox's meticulous pencil studies of the human figure, both static and in movement, were the bedrock of his painting and illustration work.

opposite
A painterly pencil study of the fall of light on people and architecture.

Kenyon Cox

opposite
Further examples of
Kenyon Cox's carefully
observed pencil studies
of the human figure, here
focusing on movement.

above
A series of head studies
from one of Cox's
sketchbooks.

Robert Crumb

In a revealing interview with *The Guardian* conducted in 2016, Robert Crumb reflected on the way in which, in the 1990s, he had suddenly been accepted at the high table of the art world. *Crumb* (1995), a documentary about his work by his friend Terry Zwigoff, had recently won the grand jury prize at the Sundance Film Festival, and he had subsequently been taken on by a swish New York gallery. 'It was like being a tramp outside a fancy restaurant,' recalled Crumb, 'watching people eat and someone suddenly says, "Come in and eat with us." I never aspired to that other world of symphony orchestras and ballet. I was the child of popular culture. I just wanted to get my work published.'

This late recognition from the rarefied world of the gallery stands in contrast to Crumb's humble upbringing and aspirations. Born in 1943 into a Catholic family in Philadelphia, Crumb endured a troubled and unhappy childhood, and he and his brothers drew and made their own comics from an early age. On leaving school, Crumb took a full-time job drawing greetings cards for American Greetings in Cleveland, Ohio. After completing hundreds of designs over four years, he left the job and spent time in Europe with his first wife, Dana Morgan, barely managing to survive on bits of freelance work for his former employers. In 1967, the year of the Summer of Love and the height of 'flower power', Crumb travelled to San Francisco.

It was there that he created *Zap Comix*. His work was already heavily influenced by his regular use of LSD, and the publication's countercultural nature soon meant that he was in great demand. The next decade was one of his most productive, resulting in his *Keep on Truckin'* cartoon and the characters Mr. Natural and Fritz the Cat, who would later appear in a highly successful animated film.

Having always felt himself an outsider, painfully rejected as an adolescent, Crumb uses his drawing skills to openly explore his preoccupations and fantasies, many of which – as his sketchbooks reveal – so brazenly swim against the tide of prevailing aesthetics and notions of acceptability.

right and opposite
Two spreads from Robert Crumb's 'Thirsty Camel' sketchbook, thought to be from 1970. Crumb's works, especially his sketchbooks, are much sought-after by collectors; those that include the use of white correction fluid, as seen here, are among the most highly prized.

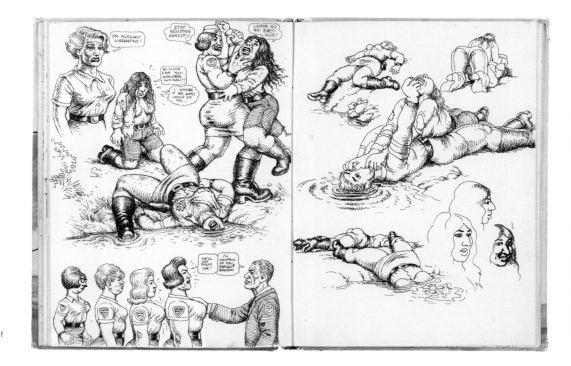

Robert Crumb

John Cuneo

John Cuneo, a highly successful, award-winning illustrator currently based in Woodstock, New York, is surprisingly and self-confessedly anxious and neurotic. Yet it is these characteristics that are perhaps key to the brilliance of his work, which can regularly be seen in such publications as the *New Yorker*, *Sports Illustrated* and *Esquire*, as well as in bespoke published collections of his drawings, including *Not Waving but Drawing: Dark Thoughts, Lightly Rendered* (Fantagraphics, 2020) and *Coping Skills: Helpful Drawings* (Fantagraphics, 2022). Here he reflects generously and frankly on his sketchbook compulsion:

'Sketchbooks feel tethered to most everything in my life these days. Both artistic progress and my mental well-being are inextricably connected to those damn little books. In fact, I hope I don't sound like a loon when I admit that daily time in a sketchbook is both a discipline and a kind of meditation around here.

'In fact, I often feel uneasy at just how dependent I am on being able to slip away into that private state of mark-making. (Am I indulging a habit at the expense of getting real work done?) I can sometimes justify things by convincing myself that all this obsessive nonsense has a legitimate purpose – perhaps I'm improving my drawing skills – but I'm not even sure that's the case. It may just be that these crowded little pages are simply an end in themselves.

'Often, the first thing drawn on a page is an (unintentional) prompt, something I'm then tempted to add to or embellish. It's like a little puzzle or an assignment I give myself: "now draw something else there, make them interact, make it a 'picture'." Maybe that's why some things look "finished" – I'm trying

to follow some self-imposed rules and not just "play" (it's been said before that I can take the fun out of most anything).

'As to "sketches" versus "drawings" or "coloured pictures", I've never been tied to the definitions of what belongs in a sketchbook. Doodles, grocery lists, phone numbers, watercolour tests, animals on bikes – it all works for me.

'I have various books scattered around the house, like a smoker trying to quit might have nicotine-gum packets next to every chair and couch. I get nervous without them close by. Sometimes I use sketchbooks as a musician might play scales – as a not entirely random warming-up, familiarizing myself with my instrument, but with a hint of purpose and practice.

'I found that I'm more comfortable drawing in a confined space and on a confined page. It sounds like a contradiction, but I feel I'm able to be more spontaneous within pre-defined borders, like a spider needs a window frame to make a web: give us too much room and we're both just flailing around in the breeze. I see a little white rectangle and something in me gets excited and says, "Oh – I can make a picture in that box!"

'When I'm fooling around in a sketchbook, it always feels that one line suggests another. A tilt of a head may dictate how the shoulders are set and then what the arms may be doing, and so on. And because of that gradational process, the "drawing" part is never entirely unconsidered. But when it comes to *what* I draw, I try and keep that as free and impulsive as possible.

'I don't always follow that urge to "finish" a sketch or to make "a picture" out of it, but

I have battled some unsavoury compulsions in my past, and colouring in these little pen drawings is by far the most benign.

'My sketchbook habit started in my twenties at a point when I was very unhappy with my commissioned illustrations, which were very influenced by other artists and felt mannered and inauthentic. I felt I needed a separate and private place to develop a more personal way of drawing my characters. I did a lot of that work (with rapidographs, crow quills and then disposable office pens) drawing in small, hardcover, spiral-bound Holbein drawing pads. I know it doesn't sound like the most liberating format, but I guess I needed fancy sketchbooks with small pages – those four walls and a little room – in order to feel comfortable wandering around. Maybe that tendency comes from my illustration background, where I'd become familiar with the confines of rules and parameters. Whatever, I filled up book after book trying to draw my way out of my old habits. (Maybe that's as good a reason as any for an illustrator to use a sketchbook.)

'As for observational drawing, most of my sketchbook work is an "inward"

opposite & page 92
John Cuneo's on-location reportage drawings of the Masters golf tournament, commissioned by *Golf Digest* magazine, demonstrate the artist's keen eye for the anecdotal – the peripheral goings-on at the edges of the tournament.

page 93
The organic nature of John Cuneo's working process is evident in the fragile, searching line that results in a nervous, gradual building-up of an image.

John Cuneo

process: what I draw in a cafe is not very different from what I draw on my couch, just more embarrassing if it's seen. But I do try to occasionally look up from my little imaginary world and mix in observational work as well. A hotel room, my studio (with dog), a very dead bumble bee on a windowsill or very alive people in an airport terminal. I made several drawings of my mother during her last days in a hospital. Those kinds of things feel like both a personal document and a coping mechanism. I'm socially awkward and sketchbooks help me function in that regard as well. That wretched creature at the Illustration Conference, hunched over in a corner and scribbling madly? That is very likely me, in my element – for better or worse.

'I was hired by *Golf Digest* magazine to do a reportage-type visual journal at the annual Masters golf tournament in Augusta, Georgia. I skulked around the course for five days with a big hat, a sketchbook and a foldable stool and made dozens of drawings, many of which were published in their original "field sketch" state in a subsequent issue.'

left
'Fox Diapers', from one of John Cuneo's sketchbooks.

opposite
Cuneo will often complete his sketchbook images, bridging the gap that so many illustrators feel exists between the idea of 'rough' and 'finished'.

pages 96–97
Apes make regular, random appearances in Cuneo's sketchbooks.

John Cuneo

John Cuneo

Histoire de Babar (1934), the first of the famous series of picturebooks featuring Jean de Brunhoff's eponymous elephant, began life as a bedtime story that De Brunhoff and his wife, Cécile, would tell their young children, Laurent and Mathieu. De Brunhoff was a painter, and his children persuaded him to make the story into a book. (It is thought that Cécile played a significant role in the creation of Babar but had her name omitted from the original author credit.) The first iteration of the book was in the form of a maquette, with very roughly drawn and loosely coloured designs mapping out the overall structure and flow of the narrative. The maquette is now held at the Morgan Library and

Museum in Manhattan, New York. It was donated by Laurent, who had continued the series following his father's death from tuberculosis in 1937, aged just thirty-seven. De Brunhoff produced a total of six Babar titles during his lifetime, although the final two had to be completed after his death, with his brother, Michel, overseeing the process and the thirteen-year-old Laurent helping to add colour to the black-and-white drawings.

Although the maquette's small size (20.5 × 15.5 cm/8 × 6 in.) contrasts with the signature large scale of many of the published editions, the rapid, sketchy studies it contains provide a valuable insight into De Brunhoff's thinking

and early character design and development. Most of the drawings have been made with graphite pencil, but there are splashes of colour too, including the red of Babar's car. Sheets of paper have been overlaid and stuck in, as a way of making changes, corrections and additions to the draft.

In his sketchbooks, De Brunhoff went on to make significant further adjustments to the content of the book. The death of Babar's mother, which had opened the story in the maquette, was dropped in favour of a less dramatic beginning, setting the scene more gently; the ending was completely overhauled as well.

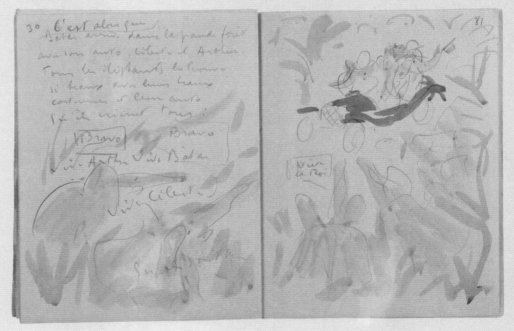

Jean de Brunhoff

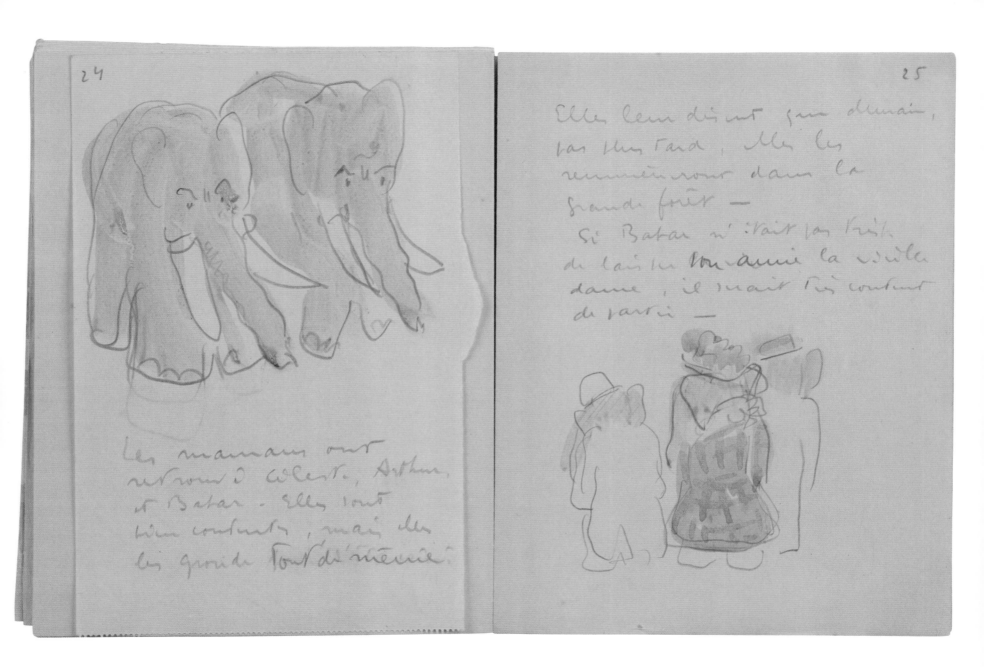

24

Les mamans ont
retrouvé Céleste, Arthur,
et Babar – Elles sont
bien contentes, mais elles
les grondent tout de même!

25

Elles leur disent que demain,
pas trop tard, elles les
ramèneront dans la
grande forêt –
Si Babar n'était pas triste
de laisser son amie la vieille
dame, il serait très content
de partir –

28

Babar part
Pour la forêt.

Les mamans voudraient
courir derrière l'auto. Elles
lèvent leur trompe tous en
par en pleur la poussière —
La ... le dame ... à son
balcon —

29

Pendant ce temps le vieux
Roi des Éléphants est mort.
après une longue maladie
Il n'a pas d'enfant et
les plus vieux des Éléphants
cherchent un nouveau
Roi —

Jean de Brunhoff

Henrik Drescher

In many ways, Henrik Drescher is a prime example of the artist/illustrator/book artist for whom sketchbooks, notebooks or journals form the foundation of their creative output. In 1967, when Drescher was twelve years old, his parents emigrated from Denmark to the United States. He studied briefly at the School of the Museum of Fine Arts, Boston, before leaving to pursue a career as an illustrator. His journals and notebooks reflect both his travels and his sometimes extremely dark visual ideas, often featuring hybrid human–animal creatures in weirdly unsettling landscapes. Some of Drescher's work also references the darker side of sexual desire, as seen in one of his most interesting books, *Turbulence* (Chronicle Books, 2001), a commercially produced artist's book complete with exquisite die-cut patterns and a range of different papers – a seductive combination of the beautiful and the perturbing. This uncompromising work has led to Drescher being seen as something of an *enfant terrible* of the illustration world, albeit a highly innovative and influential one.

At the same time, Drescher has found great success in mainstream publishing, winning several prestigious awards. In addition to producing editorial work for such leading US newspapers and magazines as the *New York Times*, the *Washington Post*, *Newsweek* and *Rolling Stone*, he has created illustrations for a number of children's picturebooks, both those he has authored himself and those he has co-written with others. Many of the picturebooks appear to draw on the European tradition of cautionary, unsentimental tales.

Drescher's own artist's books are often constructed from the piles of unused or rejected drawings that he keeps for possible later use. The drawings are often cut up, moved around and repurposed in carefully structured compositions to form new meanings, creating what he describes as 'a sort of filing system of visual material – a filing cabinet of your imagination'.

In his introduction to Chronicle Books' 2014 publication of his China sketchbooks, *China Days*, Drescher writes about living in China with his wife, Wu Wing Yee, describing it as an 'eye-opening, mind-popping experience'. He goes on to note that, 'In my time, I have attempted to be an observer and a participant. I have probably been most successful at the former ... My work, whether it be illustration, edition books, or painting, has always been about absorbing and documenting existence.'

Drescher now devotes more of his time to painting and book arts than to commercial illustration. He tells us:

'I'm not sure whether the notebooks lead to the paintings or the paintings lead to the notebooks. I've been working in books since high school; something about the perfection of the bound book as a picture container makes me happy. At this point I'm not really illustrating much; my picture-making is mainly comprised of paintings and book-works. In the past four years, I've been creating a series of removable-spread "folio" books for a collector, and the idea of working in these "non-books" frees my mind from making a "perfect" picture. Instead, it's a playground of visual ideas.'

opposite
This spread from one of Henrik Drescher's notebooks demonstrates his bold, uncompromising approach to image-making.

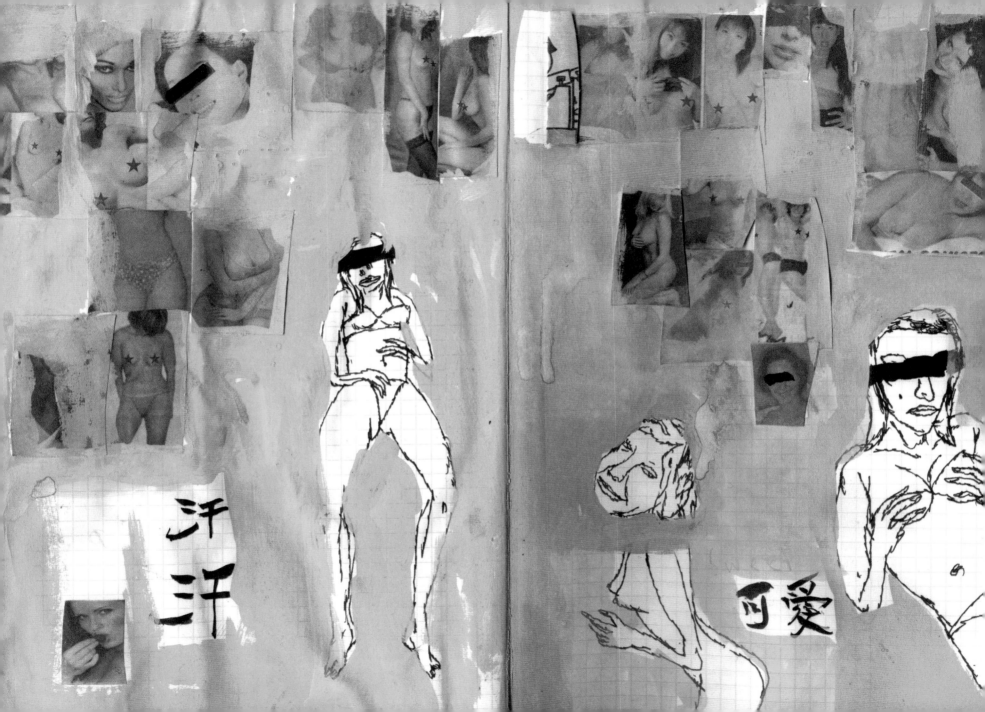

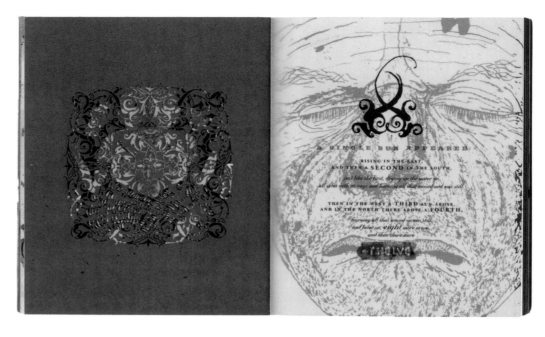

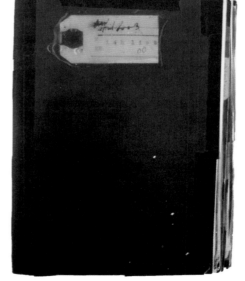

above & top right
The cover and an interior spread from Drescher's 2001 commercially produced artist's book, *Turbulence*.

right & far right
Two examples of Drescher's battered, much personalized notebook covers. Drescher describes his notebooks as comprising 'a filing cabinet of [one's] imagination'.

opposite
Drescher's notebooks incorporate drawing, painting, repurposed unused drawings, found materials and printed matter.

Illustrators' Sketchbooks

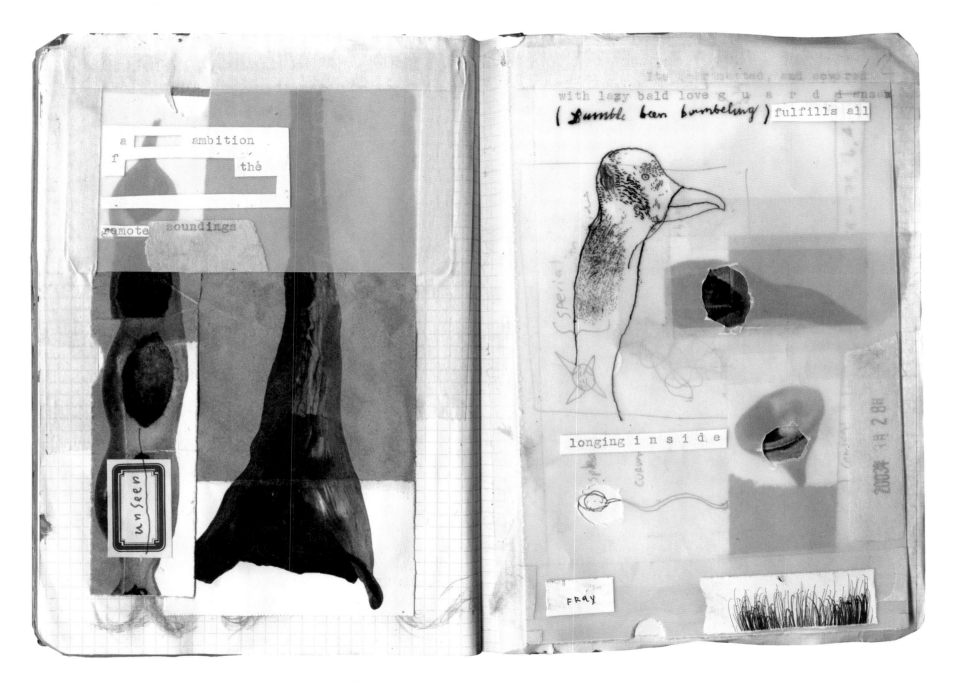

a ⬛ ambition
f   the

remote   soundings

unseen

with lazy bald love g u a r d d ense
(Bumble bean bumbeling) fulfill's all

longing i n s i d e

FRAY

Henrik Drescher

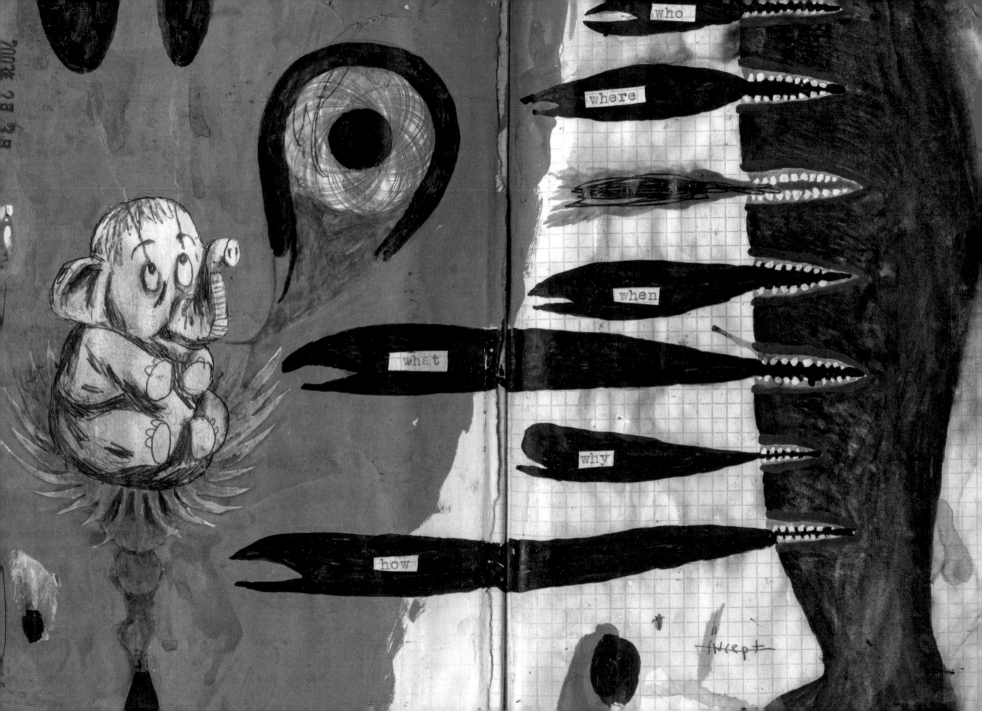

opposite
Another spread from one of Drescher's notebooks, demonstrating the variety of media and imagery employed by the artist.

right
An interior spread from *China Days*.

Henrik Drescher

Susan Einzig arrived in Britain on one of the last trains to take part in the *Kindertransport*, the rescue effort that helped to evacuate some 10,000, mostly Jewish children from Germany and surrounding central-European countries in the lead-up to the Second World War. One of a generation of artists who found refuge in Britain at this time, Einzig would eventually become an important illustrator of narrative fiction for younger readers, as well as working for such publications as *Lilliput* magazine, *Radio Times*, *Contact*, *Our Time*, and numerous advertising and design periodicals. But she will inevitably be remembered for her cover design and interior line illustrations for Philippa Pearce's classic time-slip novel, *Tom's Midnight Garden* (1958).

Suzanne, as she was known at the time, was just sixteen when she arrived in the UK, only a few months before the outbreak of war. She quickly enrolled at the Central School of Arts and Crafts. When the London art schools were relocated to Northampton, she spent some time there and became friends with the family of painter and textile designer Bernard Adeney and his wife, Noël Gilford. Later, she would work in an aircraft factory and for the War Office. After the war, Susan, as she was now known, began to pick up freelance commissions. She was also invited to teach at Camberwell School of Arts and Crafts in London, where she came under the influence of fellow teacher and illustrator John Minton. In the late 1940s, Einzig would become part of what was subsequently labelled the Neo-Romantic movement in art and illustration.

Since her death in 2009, Einzig's sketchbooks have been held by her family. Many of the early examples contain exploratory drawings for ongoing book-illustration commissions; later ones contain drawings relating to painting and prints, reflecting her main interests towards the end of her life.

Speaking to me at her home in Fulham, west London, in 2000, she began by explaining how her father had wanted her to produce fashion illustrations for the 'rag trade':

'I am hopelessly uncommercial. Instead, I drew and drew – I was really serious about that. I also discovered that I could draw out of my head, which was very exciting, and I started to illustrate stories I was reading, which happened to be Oscar Wilde's fairy stories. I have always lived in imaginative literature, which somehow seemed more real to me ... Proust said that the only real life is the life of literature. I am not unsympathetic to that idea.

'I was quickly drawn into [the Neo-Romantic] group and began to share a lot of my teaching time with Johnny [Minton]. We all used to meet at weekends and draw each other. We went to the cinema and discovered the films of Jean Renoir, René Clair and Marcel Carné ... We jived and jitterbugged to Humphrey Lyttelton's jazz band every Monday evening. We also got sucked into the drinking scene in Soho. It was all over within two or three years, but, in my memory, it seems to have been much longer.

'[Regarding *Tom's Midnight Garden*,] I had been to see the children's book editor at Oxford University Press, who had looked at my work and seemed very unsure about it. However, she gave me Philippa Pearce's manuscript to try and see if I could do it. I did two or three drawings and took them to show her, and then she asked me to do the book ... I was paid just £100 for the whole thing.'

opposite & page 110
Watercolour studies feature strongly in Susan Einzig's sketchbooks. Of these two examples, the first appears to be an unfinished study for a narrative illustration, while the second was presumably created *en plein air*.

Susan Einzig

Illustrators' Sketchbooks

below
As a book illustrator working in the age of letterpress printing, Susan Einzig was primarily trained in line drawing. Many of the sketchbook pages reflect this, whether containing drawings from observation or preparatory studies for narrative illustrations.

right
In her later years, Einzig concentrated mainly on painting and printmaking. Figures in landscapes featured strongly, as in this sketchbook drawing.

Mark Entwisle

One of the most accomplished artists in the exacting medium of watercolour, Mark Entwisle was born in Amman, Jordan. His father was in the Royal Air Force, and Entwisle was sent to boarding school in Berkshire, where his love of art as a primary means of expression flourished. Like so many artists, he found communication with words difficult, and it was not until many years later, when awareness of the condition had become more widespread, that he was diagnosed with dyslexia.

In the 1980s, Entwisle studied illustration at Brighton, where his tutors included John Vernon Lord and Raymond Briggs. After graduating, Entwisle soon discovered that his distinctively fluid approach to painting was in demand, and he began to receive commissions from many of the leading British and overseas book publishers, as well as doing editorial work, album covers and poster design. After fifteen or so years as a busy illustrator, he started to focus more on painting, in particular portraiture, and success in such competitions as the BP Portrait Award led to greater exposure in this field. In 2020, Entwisle won the Sunday Times Watercolour Competition. He now works to commission, as well as staging solo exhibitions at a leading London gallery and contributing to occasional group shows. The human figure is central to his work and features strongly in his sketchbooks.

'The importance of drawing was emphasized to us on my foundation course in Cambridge. We were encouraged to always carry a sketchbook, to make our own sketchbooks and to draw something every day ... draw anything. Consequently, I have amassed a large collection of sketchbooks, which have become journals of sorts. Looking at my drawings now I can recall other things that were happening at the time. We were told that, by drawing something, we'd understand and remember it far better than if we just looked at it with all our concentration. Sketchbooks are archives, journals ... mundane, fantastical, unfinished, practice, experiment, recollection and invention. Drawings are communications with others and yourself. To make a record or express one's thoughts, about the commonplace, the overlooked ... loved ones.

'I struggle with the written word so tend to draw at times when others would be reading ... in doctor's waiting rooms, on trains, on holiday. When I'm drawing in my sketchbooks, I'm in my element, properly looking at something. Drawing from observation ... happy to make mistakes, free of the fear of failure and more open to the possibility of chance successes.'

opposite & page 114
Family holidays for Mark Entwisle inevitably involve packing the watercolours. On a trip to Morocco, he used a landscape-format sketchbook to capture the brilliance of the colours and light, focusing on both buildings and people.

Kasbah Taorirt, Ouarzazate

Cafe de la Renaissance - Fez

Mark Entwisle

Illustrators' Sketchbooks

left
Mark Entwisle always
keeps a pocket sketchbook
at hand, allowing him
to capture moments of
waiting and watching.

Mark Entwisle

Isidro Ferrer

'Illustrator' describes just one aspect of Isidro Ferrer's prodigious and wide-ranging career. The Spaniard's oeuvre embraces not only two- and three-dimensional design but also installation, theatre design, book arts and much, much more. That his work is invariably theatrical is unsurprising: Ferrer originally studied drama, working as an actor, mime artist and scenographer for some years before an injury took him away from the stage and into graphic art. For a period of time in the late 1980s, Ferrer worked as a designer and illustrator for the Zaragoza-based newspaper *Heraldo de Aragón*. He then moved to Barcelona, where he spent a year working in the studio of the internationally acclaimed graphic designer Peret (Pere Torrent), whom Ferrer acknowledges as a major influence.

Returning to Zaragoza, Ferrer helped to establish a group design studio, Camaleón, before eventually setting up his own, working in advertising, publishing, exhibition design, television, animation and games design.

Ferrer's extraordinary creativity is served by the humble sketchbook, which underpins and supports his work. Like so many artists, he sees the sketchbook as a means of capturing visual thoughts and ideas before they escape and are lost forever.

'My memory is selective and capricious, that's why I want to put a fence around it. I insist on supporting the path of my steps with signs and marks that record the flow of traffic – milestones that mark the way, like kilometre points, and leave a record of what has been lived. My notebooks fulfil this function primarily; they are the custodian of my memory, but they are also a visual laboratory where I can bring order to the usual disorder of days and things, where I can sow ideas, I can record stimuli, where I can collect surprises.'

A principled, ethical artist and designer, Ferrer has received numerous national and international design awards. One of them, the Spanish National Design Prize for 2002, awarded by the Ministry of Science and Technology, was presented by King Juan Carlos. Rather than deliver an acceptance speech, Ferrer chose to express his opposition to the Iraq War by reading an anti-war poem. He was applauded by both the audience and the king.

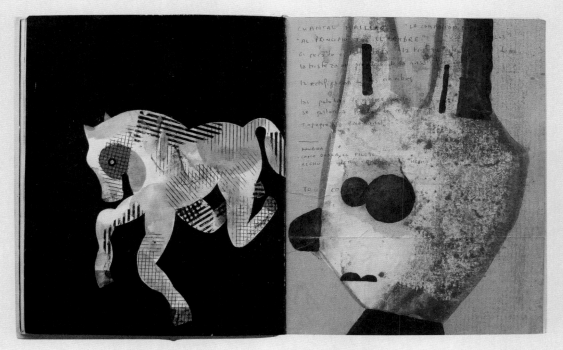

opposite, right &
pages 118–121
It could be argued that
Isidro Ferrer's sketchbooks
are works of book art in
themselves. Each one can
be read or experienced
as a kind of experimental
graphic performance – the
images working in isolation,
the entire sketchbook as
an enigmatic, suggested
narrative.

Isidro Ferrer

Con la vida a cuestas

Isidro Ferrer

LA MER À BOIRE
RUE PIAT → SUR LE PARC DE
BELLEVILLE

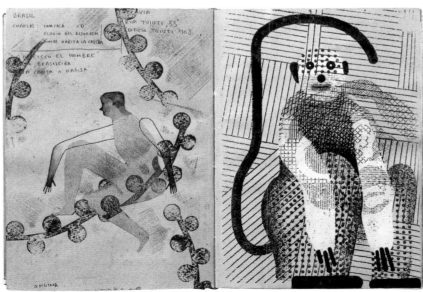

Isidro Ferrer

In a rare lengthy interview with the artist and critic Clifford Ross for *The World of Edward Gorey* (Doubleday, 1996), Gorey himself spoke of his sketchbooks as if they were a burden: 'Sometimes I feel I'd better make a very bare-bones sketch. And sometimes I can't even read the bones they're so bare.' Indeed, the contrast between the intensity and detail of Gorey's published book illustrations and the pared-back drawings of his sketchbooks is stark. This focus on structure rather than rendering is perhaps unsurprising given his background in design, specifically as a designer of book jackets – first for the publisher Doubleday, for a number of years in the early 1950s after leaving college, and then as an art director and editor at Bobbs-Merrill (which, according to the writer and art director Steven Heller, Gorey liked to call 'Boobs-Muddle').

Through his finished drawings, created by means of the unwaveringly demanding and time-consuming process of covering paper with thousands of tiny strokes of the pen that build into a tonal whole, Gorey constructed a unique, surreal world that was part American Gothic, part Edwardian dining room. It was a world in which whatever seemed to be going on 'off stage' was often at least as worrisome and disturbing as that which had visibly flowed from his pen. It was also a world that owed little to formal, academic draughtsmanship and much to a deeply literary mind. After completing only a single semester at the Art Institute of Chicago – the city in which he was born in 1925 – and spending three years as a clerk in the US Army, Gorey studied French literature

at Harvard. Throughout his career, Gorey also retained a keen interest in stage design.

In the same interview with Ross, Gorey explained that, when working on his own books, he would not start drawing until he was completely happy with the text. When Ross mentions that he has seen some of Gorey's notebooks, apparently containing drawings, notes, phrases and doodles for stories that were perhaps never completed, Gorey interjects, finishing the interviewer's sentence:

'... most of which disappear forever. Every now and then I will go through and think, "Oh, I really should do something more about that." And occasionally I may. I'm not sure about keeping notebooks, but you never know when you might want something. You might dry up completely. And then you have this little notebook that you can do something with. I used to think years ago, "Oh God, suppose I never think of anything else? Suppose nothing else ever comes to me? You better write down everything." And I still do, because I never know when I might want to use it. Now I would rather not have any new ideas. Unfortunately, I have more than I ever did before ... '

The sketchbooks shown here are from a series numbered in Roman numerals. Beginning around 1977 (the earliest visible handwritten date is 6 July 1977), the series ends with volume XVI, in which the last written date is 24 February 2000, a little under two months before Gorey's death.

opposite
Sketches for a poster and book cover for the Second International Congress of Crime Writers in 1978.

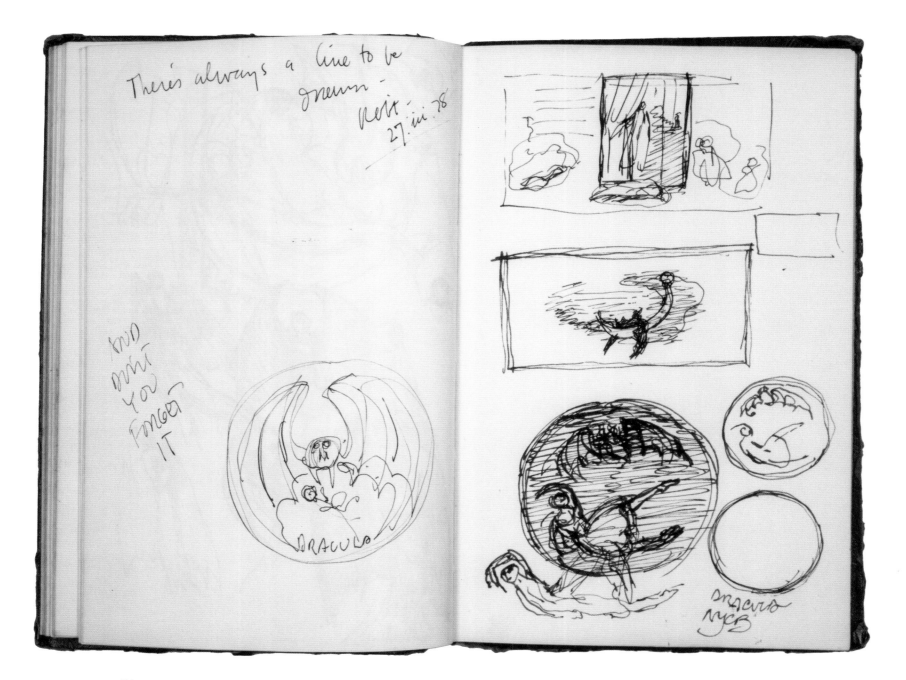

opposite

The writing at the top
of the left-hand page,
'There's always a line to
be drawn – Robt – 27.iii.78',
almost certainly refers
to Edward Gorey's close
friend Robert Greskovic,
with whom he frequently
attended performances
at the New York City
Ballet. The sketch on
the same page is of a
design created for the Broadway revival
of *Dracula* in 1977; the
design was first printed
on the rear cover of the
souvenir programme. The
sketch in the centre of the
right-hand page is for an
image used to illustrate
a couplet from William
Blake's poem 'Auguries of
Innocence'. The bottom
sketch relates to a badge
made to promote the New
York City Ballet.

**this page (clockwise
from top left)**

Sketches made for
material promoting *Gorey
Stories: An Entertainment
with Music*, which opened
at the Booth Theatre,
New York, on 30 October
1978; exploratory ideas in
a sketchbook thought to
have been started around
1981; sketches from 1996
for an unknown project;
designs for 'Kitty en Pointe',
which became a badge for
the New York City Ballet.

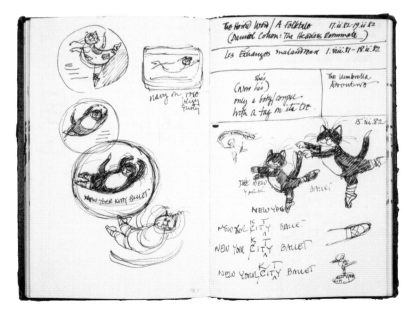

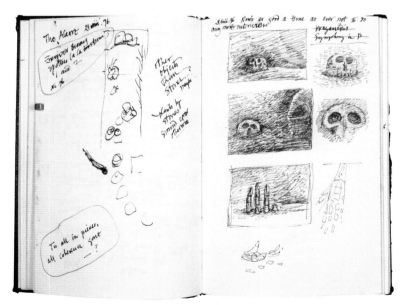

Edward Gorey

Chris Harper

Trained in both graphic design and illustration – at undergraduate and postgraduate level, respectively – Chris Harper works in all areas of communication design, including the commercial and academic sectors. His design work has encompassed, among many other things, television production, websites, advertising for print and CD covers; as an illustrator, he has worked for leading newspapers, magazines, book publishers and design groups. An apparent coming-together of design, illustration and fine art emerges from his sketchbooks, the use of which he reflects on in detail below:

'Drawing practice, whether inside or outside of the sketchbook, is central to my conceptual thinking and practice as an illustrator and designer. I use my sketchbooks to think and record visually, regarding them as an experimental space to explore the synthesis between drawing processes and the conceptualization of ideas. On a commercial and personal level, my sketchbooks serve as a place to consider the relationships that exist between materials and meaning, a space for uninhibited experimentation and visual play, where the tangible form of an idea can be given shape and purpose.

'From a background in assemblage, collage and design, developing a sketchbook habit didn't really come naturally to me. It was only when I embraced experimental drawing as my primary visual language that the self-consciousness I felt began to dissipate, and that I took ownership of my sketchbooks and drawing process. Within my sketchbooks, there is often a blurring of the boundaries between the public and the personal, the analytical and the intuitive. Much of my work finds its creative inspiration in language and text and I often create lists of ideas or themes with potential for further development or exploration. The drawing and image-making that comes as a consequence of these starting points is loose, freewheeling and at times chaotic, and I try to continually challenge myself to extend the scope and variety in my visual descriptions and my methods.

'Although the physical chronology of a sketchbook can be useful, I have also found myself at times to be limited by the physical scale of the sketchbook. At these moments, I move out of the book on to individual larger sheets of paper. This change of scale acts to focus my drawing, mark-making and compositional thinking. I progressively rework and edit these preparatory studies until I reconcile the image and idea. As a consequence, my sketchbooks can often feel like disjointed scrapbooks, filled with fragmentary drawings and collages culled from other sources and assembled with a coherence that, at times, only I can read and visually interpret.

'My current practice as an illustrator moves continually between analogue and digital processes. As my work has changed and developed, moving from analogue to digital final outcomes, so too have my sketchbook methods. In the past, I developed my roughs to be more resolved and concrete and [to therefore] enable my subsequent focus to be on painting alone. Now my sketchbook thumbnails are quicker and more urgent in their description. I draw more readily, expressively and variously from reference, exploring character, posture and gesture in order to build a bank of imagery and mark-making that, when scanned, can be digitally composited to create the final artwork. When editing and assembling my artwork, I strive to retain the physicality, vitality and materiality of these sketchbook drawings as they have the potential to imbue the final image with an authenticity it might lack otherwise. If this digital materiality – qualities that characterize my current personal exploration and commissioned work – is visible in the artwork, I believe that the starting point for this will invariably be found in my initial drawing and sketchbook practice.'

opposite & pages 128–131
Chris Harper's sketchbooks incorporate mark-making experiments, experimental drawing and typography. A strong sense of graphic construction is evident throughout.

SCARED

SACRED.

Chris Harper

Illustrators' Sketchbooks

Chris Harper

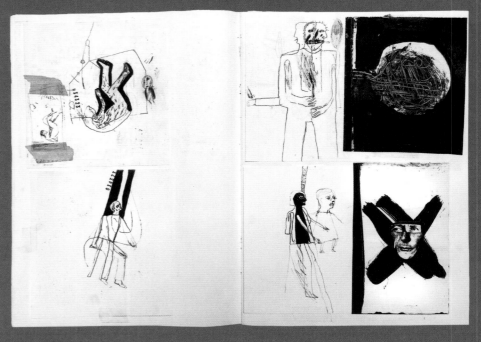
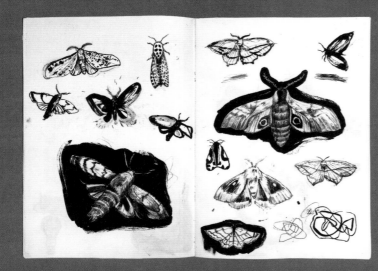

Illustrators' Sketchbooks

Chris Harper

Standing in Jon Harris's splendidly chaotic studio-cum-home in the historic waterfront area of King's Lynn, Norfolk, surrounded by paintings in progress, it soon becomes clear that there is one thing and one thing only that is perfectly organized: the shelf holding his sketchbooks. A lifetime's worth stand in an orderly line, each one carefully dated on its spine (with both start and finish dates) in white acrylic ink. When a sketchbook is removed from the shelf, more white ink is revealed in the form of decorative titling on the front and a detailed listing of the contents on the back. Harris tells me that this indexing is important in case he needs a reference for a painting or illustration.

Harris's sketchbooks document his life, his travels and his obsessions; wherever he goes, his sketchbook goes too. Their pages are filled predominately with observational drawings, especially of architectural and mechanical subjects – buildings going up or coming down, views from his window, farm machinery, aeroplanes, typography, the human figure, the bloke driving the bus, and the occasional set of preparatory drawings and designs for illustration commissions. The overwhelming majority of the drawings are rendered in black ink, courtesy of his collection of ancient Rotring drawing pens, the tips carefully filed down to form a 45-degree angle. Here and there, the quickly jotted-down and heavily annotated visual information is interrupted by an intensely observed double-page land- or cityscape, rendered in black and white with a painter's eye, somehow magically evoking tone, colour, air and light.

Harris was born in 1943 in the English county of North Staffordshire. His father was an engineer with origins in New Zealand and, in recent years, Harris has travelled there to

reconnect with the wider family. As a child, he attended a leading public school but found it an unhappy place. One day, however, a new art teacher arrived by the name of Graham Drew, who, recalls Harris, 'revolutionized the lives he touched' – his own among them. Other influences include the ubiquitous Adrian Hill 'how to paint' books and an art manual by a certain Dr J. G. Garrett, 'a leisure sketcher in pen'. The latter, says Harris, was of particular significance, although he has searched for a copy unsuccessfully for many years. It was Harris's art teacher, Mr Drew, who encouraged him not to apply to art school but to follow his passion for architecture. He subsequently gained a place at the School of Architecture at Cambridge University, where he was taught by the artist, writer and great-grandson of Charles Darwin, Christopher Cornford, and the artist, designer and typographer Edward Wright, whom Harris credits with his love of letterforms.

Over the years, Harris has worked for the National Trust, contributed topographical illustrations and illustrated maps for a range of magazines and publications, served on and advised various architectural preservation bodies, and taught part-time at several educational institutions, including art schools. In 1997, the Fitzwilliam Museum in Cambridge staged a major retrospective of his work, which Harris describes as serving to demonstrate to his then ailing parents that he 'wasn't a total flop'.

The sketchbooks are at the heart of everything Harris has done. 'They are', he says, 'like a family member. They should stay together.'

opposite
Jon Harris's interest in architecture, construction and demolition has led him to record changes in the built environment.

page 134
Throughout his life, Harris has observed and drawn the human figure – both in weekly life-drawing classes and 'in the field' – in the form of anecdotal studies of everyday life (top left and bottom right). He has also had a lifelong fascination with machines; the sketches shown here (bottom left and top right) were made at a country fair.

page 135
A 1970s Rotring pen might not be the obvious tool for describing light and tone, but in this drawing of Houghton Mill in Cambridgeshire, Harris employs a range of marks to capture the subtle effects of light.

page 136
Many of Harris's sketchbooks contain studies and working notes for a range of illustration commissions, for illustrated maps, tour guides and the like.

page 137
Harris's interest in machines, both old and new, is evidenced by the many sketchbook pages filled with drawings and colour studies. This one was made during a visit to an air museum.

Illustrators' Sketchbooks

Ely cathedral park, quick notes for new path up through the Ripon Minster churchyard 2-IV-16 30 mins.

Jon Harris

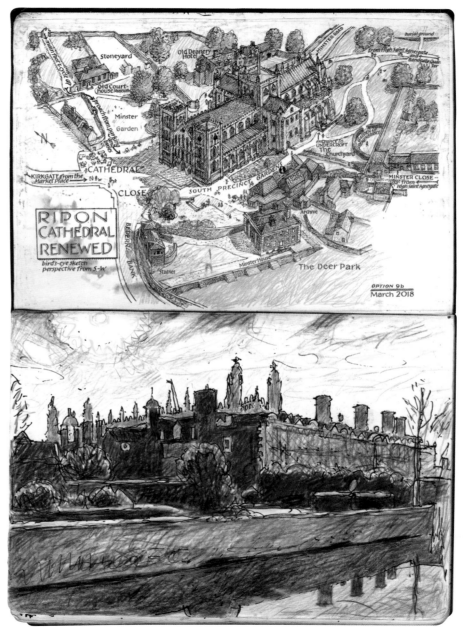

Illustrators' Sketchbooks

Handley Page Victor at Duxford late morning Sunday 13th March 2016 — a different sense of human geometry, framed by AirSpace

Jon Harris

Hergé

Georges Prosper Remi, known universally as Hergé, based his pen name on the French pronunciation of his initials in reverse, 'RG'. Speaking to Jacques Chancel on French radio in 1979, he explained with typical modesty why, at the age of nineteen, he had chosen to use a pseudonym: 'I thought that one day perhaps, after much practice, I would become a good artist. While waiting to become one, I hid behind a pseudonym, saying to myself that perhaps one day I would sign my real name.' His most successful creation, *The Adventures of Tintin* series, would become a global industry. Twenty-three volumes were published between 1929 and the early 1980s, the first completed when he was just twenty-two. A twenty-fourth volume, unfinished at the time of his death in 1983, was published in 1986.

Born in relatively humble circumstances in Brussels in 1907, Hergé would become one of those rare things: an illustrator who can genuinely lay claim to being a household name. It is a measure of his international acclaim that his works are now held in a magnificent, purpose-built museum: the Musée Hergé in Louvain-la-Neuve, to the south of Brussels, designed by the architect Christian de Portzamparc and opened in 2009. Such grandeur and status could hardly have been on the young artist's mind when he set to work on his first comic strip. Published in the highly conservative scouting magazine *Le Boy-Scout Belge*, the cumbersomely titled *The Extraordinary Adventures of Totor, Patrol Leader of the Maybugs* first appeared in 1926. Although

Hergé was still in his teens, his skill as an artist was abundantly clear. The influence of silent film was especially noticeable at this time; the young Hergé was a keen cinema-goer, and it would be another year before *The Jazz Singer* arrived from Hollywood with its early version of a soundtrack. Totor is now seen as the prototype for Tintin, his mop of hair eventually evolving into the familiar Tintin quiff. The rest, as they say, is history.

The burgeoning success of *The Adventures of Tintin* meant that it became increasingly difficult for Hergé to meet demand. In 1950, he founded Studios Hergé, building up a team of trusted artist friends to assist with production – an arrangement, one could argue, firmly in the tradition of the great Flemish painters of the seventeenth century and their studios. The many sketches and storyboards that happily survive, and which are housed at the Musée Hergé, provide a fascinating insight into the working processes of Hergé and, later, his team. Were it not for the fact that we know when they were created, the clean lines and immaculate flat colour washes of the final printed artworks could easily be mistaken for having been produced digitally. The mass of developmental sketches shows us how painstakingly Hergé studied posture and gesture, making multiple sketches of his characters and their interactions with one another to work out how to convey their reactions, moods and emotions through body language and facial expression. The final artworks are only the tip of an iceberg of research and exploratory drawing.

opposite & pages 140–143
The numerous exploratory pencil lines of the preparatory drawings of Hergé, and later of his studio team, reveal much about the 'skeleton' of draughtsmanship that supports and contrasts with the clean lines of the finished illustrations.

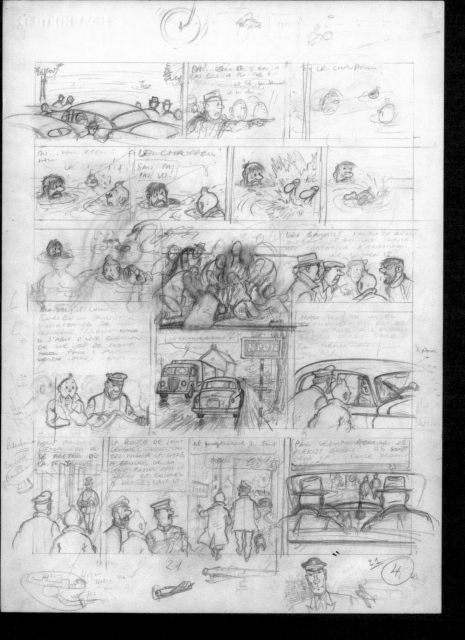

Katsushika Hokusai

Universally associated with the woodblock print *The Great Wave* (*c*. 1830–32), reproductions of which have adorned the walls of living rooms the world over, Katsushika Hokusai in fact produced more than thirty thousand artworks over his long and somewhat eccentric life. He is thought to have been born in October 1760 (he was unsure of his own birth date) and died in May 1849. 'Hokusai', meaning 'North Studio', is the name he kept for the longest period of his life, having changed it numerous times – a practice that was common in Japan at the time. He also, famously, moved home and studio repeatedly, apparently because of an aversion to cleaning. Each time the accumulation of dirt became intolerable, he would move on.

As a teenager, Hokusai became an apprentice in a woodcarver's studio and was trained as a block-cutter, learning the practical skills that he would soon apply with such vision and sensitivity. He was supervised by Katsukawa Shunshō, the leading designer of prints of kabuki actors, which were in great demand. In Japan at that time, there was a strict division of labour in the production of prints. A designer provided the initial design, which was then worked up in more detail by a copyist. The resulting drawing was then cut by the block-cutter before the completed woodblock was printed by a team of trained printers. It was not until the early twentieth century that artists began to take on the entire process, from design to print, as was common in the West.

In the early years of the nineteenth century, Hokusai concentrated mainly on book illustration. *Hokusai's Manga*, a series of instruction books filled with thousands of simplified drawings, explained how to draw everything from a wild boar to self-defence techniques. The series was extremely successful and helped ease the artist's financial woes. The word 'manga', now associated with popular Japanese comics, graphic novels and animated films, has its origins in the Chinese word 'manhua', meaning 'whimsical' or 'impromptu' drawing.

The prints shown here are from Hokusai's book *Shashin gwafu* (variously translated as 'Realistic Sketchbook', 'Pictures Drawn from Nature' or 'Sketches Drawn from Life'). It was published in 1814, the same year in which the first of Hokusai's *Manga* series was released. In contrast to the *Manga* books, however, *Shashin gwafu* was carefully produced to show the very best qualities of the artist's work. Published in a limited edition, the book can be found in the collections of some of the world's finest museums and galleries.

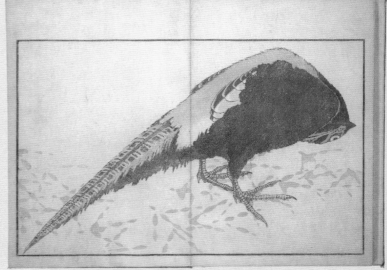

Katsushika Hokusai

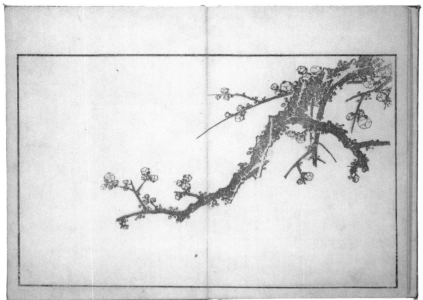

opposite
The covers of Hokusai's
Shashin gwafu, complete
with a study of lizards
on the back. The book
measures 26 cm (10 in.)
in height.

this page
Hokusai's prints display
the artist's trademark
elegance of design and
use of white/negative
space, as in the snowy
lakeside village scene
(top left).

Katsushika Hokusai

Born in Tainan, Ya-Ling Huang originally studied fine art at Taichung University of Education. During this time, she began to realize that her primary interests were in fact in storytelling and illustration. She undertook her postgraduate studies in the UK, receiving commendations in the Macmillan Prize for Children's Book Illustration, the Bologna Illustration Exhibition and the 'Well-Designed Book' competition in Katowice, Poland. At the same time, Huang was developing highly atmospheric graphic novels and wordless books, sometimes dealing with the bleaker side of urban life. Now permanently based in England, her focus is mainly on creating picturebooks, both as author-illustrator and in collaboration with such leading authors as Vivian French.

Huang has been widely published in both Asia and the English-speaking world by the likes of Frances Lincoln, Kids Can Press and Walker Books. Throughout her work, in both sketchbook and published form, there is a strong sense of empathy and kindness between the characters, whether they be humans or animals. Generally, such qualities are primarily rooted in and flow from the personality of the artist; in Huang's case, they can also be traced to the many sketchbooks she has filled with direct observations of people, closely watching their gestures and interactions. The resulting knowledge has

been subtly absorbed and transferred into animal characters, which she draws and paints repeatedly in her sketchbooks, and which feature strongly in her published books.

'During my studies, I was encouraged to do as much drawing as I could and was able to explore a variety of materials during observational drawing, such as acrylic, marker pens, collage, pencils and watercolours. Later, I found my passion in mixed materials applied to my final artwork – watercolours, coloured pencils and a bit of collage in particular.

'When I started to create picturebooks, I realized that I had never had an animal character as a protagonist and I drew so little of them. To challenge myself, I decided to draw a lot of animals in my sketchbooks and also practised animal characterization that can eventually be useful in my work. During that time, I was exploring the relationship between lines and shapes of colour and trying to find a balance between them. Creating outlines with watercolour brushes was something I liked a lot because it created delightful and bold textures that felt like something unique in watercolour. That probably explains why my first book [*This Is the Way in Dogtown*, Frances Lincoln, 2020] is all about dogs and is in that medium.'

opposite & pages 150–151
Drawing from direct observation has always played a significant role in Ya-Ling Huang's illustration practice, with a particular focus on urban living. She also uses her sketchbooks to experiment with anthropomorphic character design (page 151, bottom left) – making links between the observed and the imagined.

Collier Road in the morning
4.38 am 7 oct 2014
wake up for toilet
CB1 2AH   Cambridge
Jade

Ya-Ling Huang

WAITING, CYCLING WALKING PEOPLE
ON REGENT ST PIZZA HUT

12.04 PM 19 Oct 2014
on Regent St.
Cambridge

Ya-Ling Huang

Tove Jansson

The importance of Tove Jansson's contribution to the field of illustration and to the broader world of art and literature has become increasingly apparent since her death in 2001. Primarily celebrated for her creation of the Moomins, the strangely white, rounded trolls whose world was explored in eight novels, five picturebooks and one short-story collection, Jansson went on to write a number of novels for older readers and to receive multiple international cultural awards, including, in 1966, the prestigious Hans Christian Andersen Award for Writing.

In 2014, in Jansson's native Finland, a major exhibition at the Ateneum Art Museum in Helsinki was staged in celebration of the centenary of her birth, attracting more than 300,000 visitors before travelling to Japan, where her work has long enjoyed a devoted following. The first major UK exhibition of her work as a painter, illustrator and cartoonist was held at the Dulwich Picture Gallery in south London in 2017. Today, Finland boasts a permanent home for many of the artworks of one of the country's most famous exports. Opened on 17 June 2017, the purpose-built Moomin Museum houses the collection of Moomin artwork that Jansson originally donated to the Tampere Art Museum in 1986.

Jansson's illustrated sketchbook-diaries offer a fascinating glimpse into the private world of the Moomins' creator. Shown here are extracts from her teenage diaries and some early storyboards for Moomin strips.

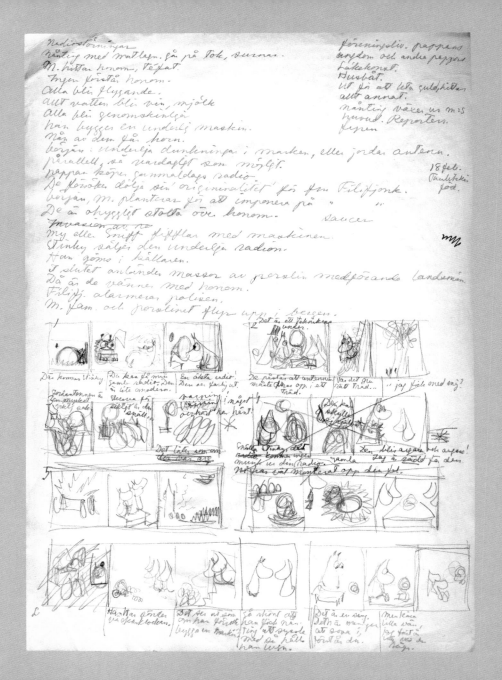

Hur det kändes när jag klätt-rade opp i "Guineas" rigg, i mina skinn-byxor.

"En ung mansperson med bya utseende." Men jag tyck-te mer om den andra. Hans ögon var alldeles ljus-ljusblå och hans näsa såg mystisk och knölig ut. Jag tyckte att hans hår var litet rött och det krulla-de sig på honom i en massa små lockar.
"Va vill ni?" undrade den gamla (skepparen)
"Vi skall titta vad det är för en skuta, å hälsa på," svarade jag. De frågade om det fanns mjölk att köpa och sen om det fanns sprit och så fick vi komma ombord. Sanden kördes från strand på en lång smal bräda och när jag gick över flaxade skinnbyxor-na om benen som stora vingar.
Jag måste beskriva mina skinnbyxor, som jag sydde under vintern, för jag älskar dem. Baktill och fläckvis framtill har jag kattskinn och på sidorna långhårigt vitt getskinn från Annas krage. Benena är av miss-tag litet trånga upptill och hemskt breda nertill, och de är av grått getskinn med vitt krulles på insidan och långa tafsar framtill. På vänstra benet är en bit svart kaninskinn. Det är klart att alla Pellingbor blir förbluffade över dem och det blev naturligtvis också de på Guinea. Jag fick komma ner i den lilla lilla kajutan med Pråle och sen undersökte vi hela skutan. I för'n fanns en kåstrika och som räddningsboj hade de en gammal Fordring. Men den flöt inte alls. De sade att man måste äta vara sill på havet annars drunknar man, men det tror jag inte. Så börja den yngsta skryta med hur bra han

right
A diary entry from August
1929. On the left-hand
page, the note at the
bottom of the drawing
reads, 'I'm sitting and
philosophizing in the
apartment.' On the right-
hand page, Jansson writes
about what she did at
the end of the summer.
Her last school year is
about to begin, and she
wonders what will happen
after that, including if she
will continue to write in
her journal. The drawings
are captioned, 'Tove in
the Countryside becomes
Tove in the City'.

opposite
This diary entry dates from
May 1931. Jansson is now
studying in Stockholm, and
she shows herself painting
in her attic room, lost in
concentration and very
nervous. A man called
Brantberg comes to look
at her painting and tells
her she uses too much
colour and should apply
to the Academy.

rigig, Lena, en "uppenbarelse i himmelsblått."
skildes med pussar. Jag tittar vidare.
Och så lustigt! Här sitter jag i uggleträt med en
sockerdricka och "kungen av Klondyke — och
säger: "Ja, jag är lycklig nu." —
På nästa sida försöker jag jobba. Men det är
lönlöst, då som nu, "min energi har gått dit
döda krabbor gå..."
Och här: "högre, med sina hemska ynglingar
med svajigt hår och sköna, styva, unga damer
förskräcker mig...." Det är väl festligt!
Så läser jag vidare om Pellinge, "stugan som
luktade sur limpa och bass, med jämrande
golv och rosenknoppade gardiner" — "solen,
som står lik ett rött öga över skötbåten."
mamma sätter papperstrutar över tomatplantor-
na, så att de liknar små vita flickor i mörkret."
Och så blir jag alldeles hemsjuk och sentimental, och tigger och suckar och bedrar mig själv,
och glömmer, att det säkerligen kommer en
tid, då jag längtar mig sjuk efter detta lilla
rummet — där luften är tung av cigarettrök
och grubbel och gamla förtroenden och löften.
Fy fan! — Nu skall jag opp o hoppa!
Söndagen är en bra uppfinning — utom när
en lurar en till att ligga och skriva smör-
ja, och trassla in sig i motsägelser. Hej!

Ja tänk, det är 10 nde maj och jag lever, och hoppas
på något roligt än — och nära är det till pingsten.
    Jobbar i jämn takt - puk-a-puk — bara nu och
då ett litet energiryck, men oftare saktar jag av
i farten och går opp
och sätter mig på Pek-
nis tak, och röker, och
äter min lunch, och lä-
ser "morden vid Caulfield
Gardens" — och spänstar
i mina nya overalls
tills jag trillar ner.
I dag höll jag på med en
temperamålning som intres-
serade mig mycket.
Arg som ett bi förstås — rädd för eventuella hånfull-
la kritiker, fäng opp över öronen och i pytsar på tre
m:s omkrets, slarvar iväg i vild fart, illröd och
nervös — kort sagt, sådan jag är när nånting
intresserar mig. Kom Brantberg. Ställde sig
bakom och bara titta. Jag kröp ihop, slickade
ideli distraktion och nervositet på penseln och
fick halsen full av formalin. "Fröken." sade Brantberg. "Sätter på för mycket
färg." Paus.
Sedan: "Sök in i Akademin.
Det är skäl till det."
Sade och försvann.
Nu är jag så stolt
så det nästan verkar
obehagligt. För det är,

Oliver Jeffers

A tour through the sketchbooks of Oliver Jeffers reveals a veritable torrent of ideas and creativity. A pioneering superstar of the new age of authorial illustrator-painters, Jeffers's apparently limitless artistic energy extends across picturebook-making, gallery painting, installation and more. His output is increasingly ambitious, and increasingly nimble in its ability to sidestep attempts to categorize it in terms of 'fine' or 'commercial' art. Each of his works is driven by a desire to communicate fundamental ideas, to provoke thought and reflection, and, as Jeffers himself puts it, 'to share the wonderment of the question they pose or answer they suggest, never to prove yourself worthy of some demanded contemplation'. Among his more unusual projects is *Our Place in Space*, a collaboration with Professor Stephen Smartt inviting people to take a wider view of their place in the universe by means of a touring, Jeffers-designed scale model of the solar system, an interactive app, and various educational events.

Jeffers's sketchbooks play an important role in all of his creative ventures, acting as a repository for ideas, both formed and unformed, and graphic fragments. In 2002 and 2008, Jeffers, who divides his time between Brooklyn and his native city of Belfast, engaged in a collaborative project with two New York-based artists, Mac Premo and Duke Riley, and Jeffers's older brother, Rory, a long-term collaborator. The project involved the participants passing a single black sketchbook among themselves, each artist having five days to complete a spread in response to the previous contribution before sending the sketchbook to the next person in the chain, without any other communication. Since the artists were in different continents, the sketchbook travelled tens of thousands of miles. The project was called *Book*.

Jeffers's own sketchbooks are often in the form of old logbooks or accounting books, which provide an already slightly distressed surface rather than a pure white page. Occasionally, his visual ideas are expressed entirely through drawing; more often, however, they are delivered through a range of media, including collage (composed of various forms of found graphic ephemera, such as photographs and typography), paint, ink and pencils. Here is visual thinking at its most acute, with the artist unlocking the graphic power of apparently mundane, everyday objects and putting them in collision with expressions of movement, speech, thought, signs and signals to comment on politics, the environment and any of the other major issues facing the human race.

below, opposite & pages 158–159
Behind the tattered cover boards of his sketchbooks can be found Oliver Jeffers's world of graphic ideas. The politics of his native Northern Ireland are heavily present in the pages shown here.

Lesson
I wil`
Pict

Illustrators' Sketchbooks

Charles Keeping

Charles Keeping was one of the finest illustrators of the twentieth century. Indeed, one of his tutors at the Regent Street Polytechnic School of Art, the illustrator and printmaker Nigel Lambourne, once said of him, 'He was the most natural draughtsman I ever saw or worked with.' A proud Londoner, Keeping was born in 1924 to a working-class family in the Lambeth Market area of the city. The modest home in which he grew up had a small backyard that looked on to a large, bare brick wall, alongside which could be seen carthorses. Keeping was fascinated by these animals and would stare endlessly at them. Later, the motifs of intricately rendered brick walls and acutely observed horses would feature throughout his work as an artist. Lambourne also recalled (in conversation with Keeping's biographer, Douglas Martin) that his student would often seem to be 'dashing off' his drawings while chatting to the life model or looking around distractedly, yet the result was 'anything but superficial' and was invariably 'all there'.

Keeping had drawn obsessively since early childhood and longed to go to art school. However, when his father died while he was still a teenager, and with a sister still at school, he needed to earn a living and so became an apprentice at a local printing company. Fortunately, such a position was also known to be a route by which a gifted young artist could get to college. His ambitions were fired further when, as part of his apprenticeship, he was sent to collect artworks from illustrators and deliver them to the printer.

After serving four years in the Royal Navy during the Second World War, Keeping gained a part-time place at Regent Street Poly, supporting himself by working as a 'gas man', entering the Victorian slum homes of North Kensington and Paddington to read meters. This experience would also find its way into his work, including a commission to illustrate a selection of Charles Dickens's books for the Folio Society. From the late 1950s, Keeping became part of a 'golden generation' of British book illustrators, which included Brian Wildsmith, John Burningham and Raymond Briggs. His consummate draughtsmanship and graphic flair brought him a flood of commissions alongside his own, highly innovative picturebook concepts, many of which can now be seen as being way ahead of their time.

Keeping died in 1988. His family home in south London now houses a gallery of his work, together with that of his artist wife, Renate. Keeping's sketchbooks clearly support the recollections of his old tutor Lambourne. Across his sketchbooks and notebooks as a whole, there are relatively few surviving examples of observational drawing. Many of them are shown here. Later books seem to have been used mostly for information-gathering and very rough sketches for book illustrations, establishing composition and structure. In every case, however, they exhibit all the confidence and bravado that we might expect from such a master.

opposite & pages 162–165
Taken from some of Charles Keeping's very early sketchbooks, these spreads demonstrate clearly how his virtuoso draughtsmanship and signature illustrative vocabulary were forged through constant observation of his favourite subjects: horses, working-class people, London – and more horses.

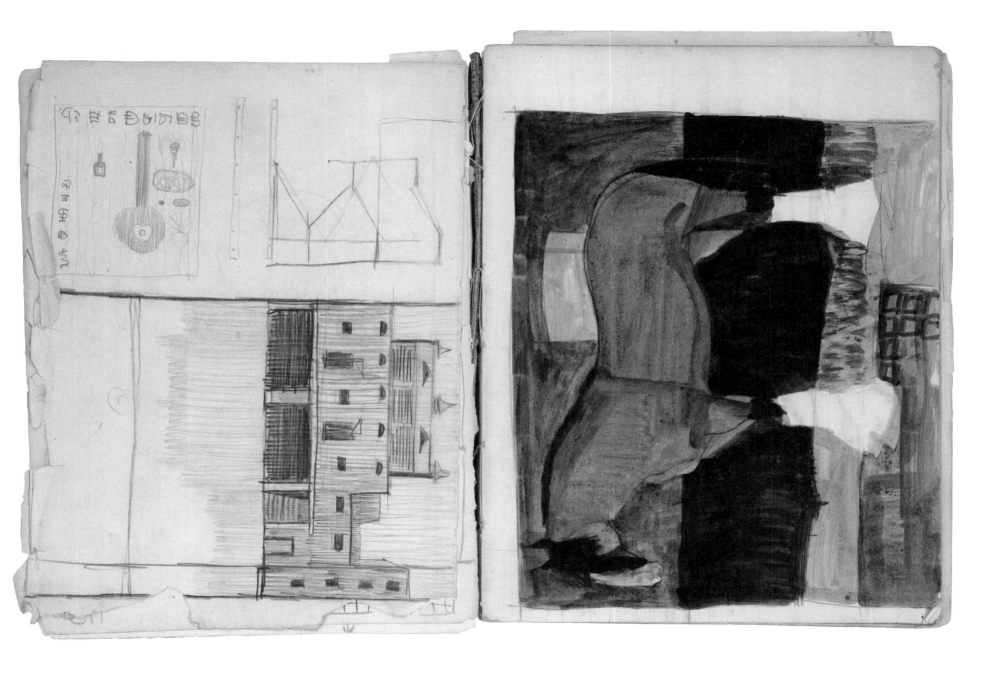

Charles Keeping

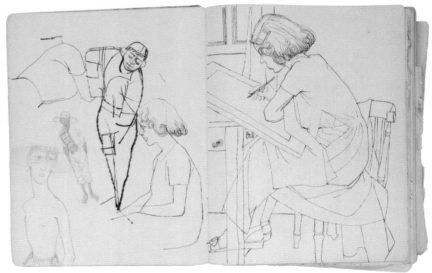

This old horse outside Green Park in 1953

I actually bought this horse in 1971, she was called Mary, a lovely old mare, but I sold her for slaughter, owing to bad feet in 1974. She was at least 25 years old.

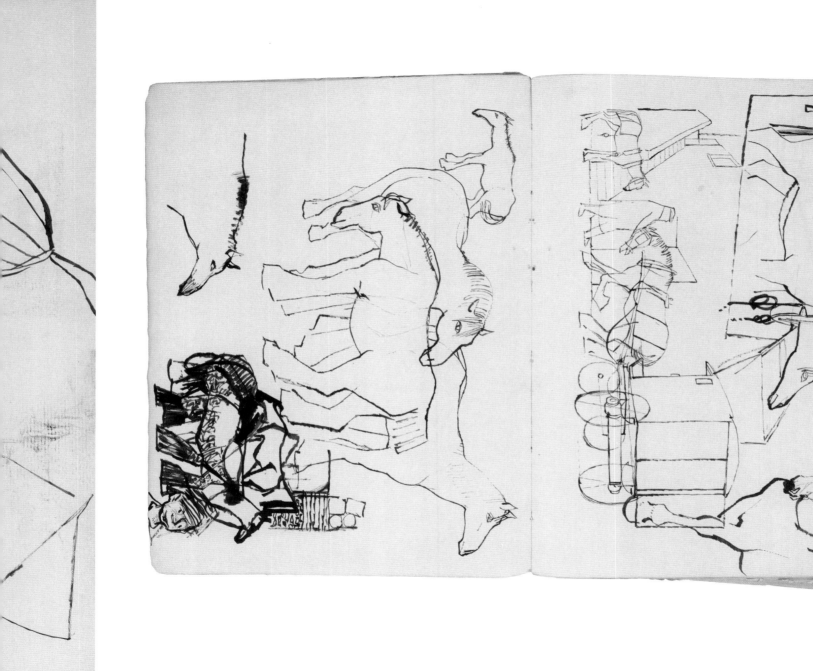

Charles Keeping

The rows of sketchbooks that line the bookshelves of John Lawrence's studio fight for space with multiple copies of the more than two hundred books he has illustrated over the last seventy or so years. Born in Hastings in 1933, Lawrence was sent at an early age to a Catholic boarding school further inland, in the hope that he would be safe from the German bombs that were beginning to fall on English coastal towns. He remembers first starting to draw while still a young boy: 'I'd spend hours and hours poring over Walt Disney images and copying them. I was fascinated by the way Donald Duck's beak would curve up at the end, and I suppose I was teaching myself to draw. And of course the comedy side interested me as well.'

After school, Lawrence enrolled at Hastings College of Art, the principal of which was the lithographer and watercolourist Vincent Lines. After doing his National Service in West Africa, Lawrence was determined to get a place at a London art school and was accepted at the Central School of Arts and Crafts. In his typically self-effacing manner, he suggests that the unusual and exotic subject matter of his sketchbook drawings from his time in Africa may have influenced the interviewers' decision. While in the queue to enrol at Central, Lawrence found himself talking to John Burningham, who would remain a lifelong friend.

Although Lawrence is perhaps best known for his illustrations derived from wood engravings, many of his published illustrations appear to have grown seamlessly from his sketchbook drawings. Some notable examples include his illustrations for the original edition of *Watership Down* by Richard Adams (1972) and the Cranks restaurant cookery books. For all these highly successful publications, the greater part of the work involved Lawrence drawing in sketchbooks on location, with many of the resulting drawings used directly as illustrations or with only minor amendments. 'For the Cranks books,' he explains, 'I would visit the various venues and draw directly on the spot – the interiors and their inhabitants, other food-related environments. Similarly, for *Watership Down*, I would visit Richard Adams in Hampshire and we would go off walking around the actual places where the story was set. He would point out the specific spots that inspired him. I did draw rabbits there from observation too, but of course these had to be developed more in the studio.'

When on holiday, Lawrence finds he is unable to 'settle' until he has taken his sketchbook out of his famous shoulder bag. 'I've always felt I had to be working all the time, being freelance ... feeling that I've got to be "on top of my game". But also, as I'm stuck working in the studio all the time, I feel the need to go out and actually look at the everyday anecdotal stuff – the real world.'

opposite
John Lawrence has always taken a sketchbook on holiday with him. This one, from a trip to Turkey, is typically full of anything from everyday life that catches his voracious eye.

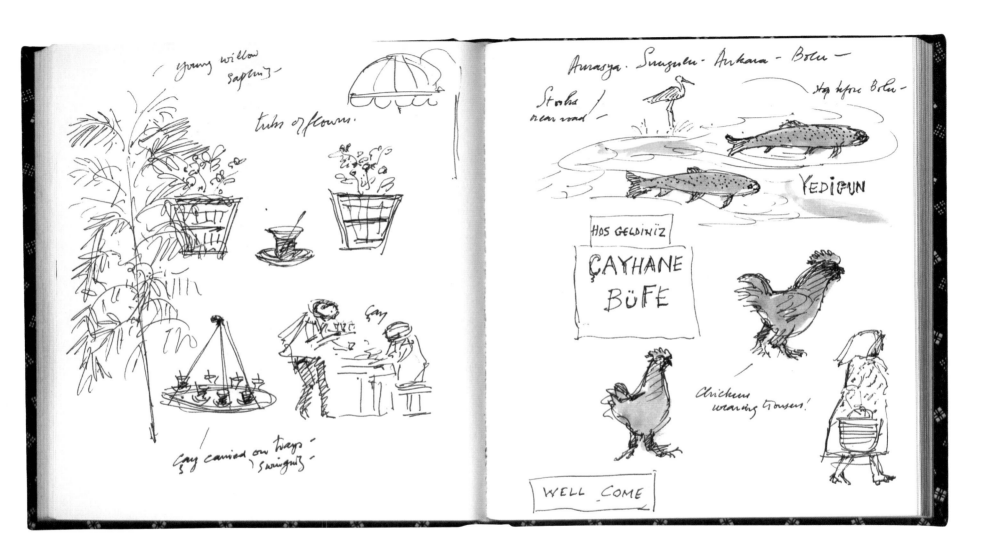

young willow sapling -

tubs of flowers.

Çay carried on trays - swinging -

Amasya. Suzuni - Ankara - Bolu -

Storks near road -

stop before Bolu -

YEDIGUN

HOS GELDINIZ
ÇAYHANE
BÜFE

Chickens wearing trousers!

WELL COME

John Lawrence

Santo Spirito

hot
mustardy
colour!

These studies of Piazza
Santo Spirito in Florence,
one of John Lawrence's
favourite destinations, were
created using line and
wash with coloured pencil.

Santo
Spirito

orange fruit

orange

ochre naples
yellow

FARMACI

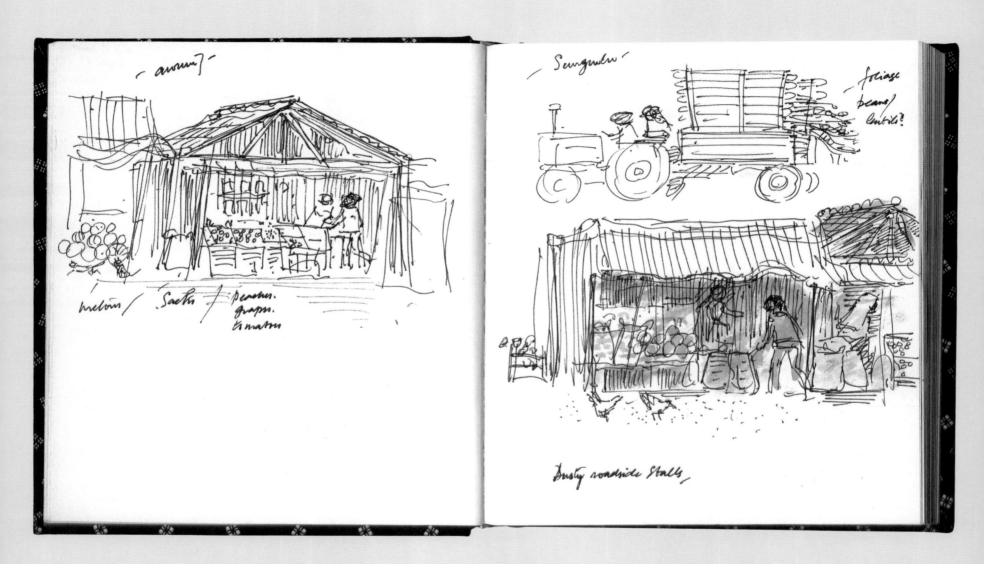

avocado

melons   _Sacks_   _peaches._
grapes.
tomatoes

Seingwelu

foliage beans / lentils?

Dusty roadside stalls,

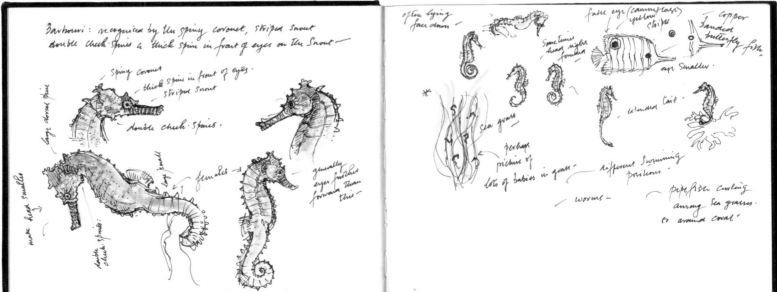

opposite
A second spread from John Lawrence's Turkey sketchbook.

right
In addition to filling his sketchbooks with observational drawings, Lawrence uses them for research and development while working in the studio on book illustration. These pages show meticulous studies for a Folio Society edition of *The Seeing Stone* (2009), the first book in Kevin Crossley-Holland's 'Arthur Trilogy', and for Chris Butterworth's *Sea Horse* (Walker Books/Candlewick, 2015).

John Lawrence

An unusual combination of pure observation and imaginary characters can be found in the sketchbooks of Shih-yu Lin. Improbably, both these things can sometimes find themselves inhabiting the same image. An acutely observed drawing of an urban street scene might be invaded by alien comic creatures – driving vans, riding bicycles, drinking coffee, or just hanging out. Now and then, an outbreak of naked dancers will populate a spread or two, adopting highly dramatic poses, as if expressing joy in their rebellious nudity. According to Shih-yu, such dancers tend to appear when he is feeling stressed, perhaps helping to release some tension on the illustrator's behalf.

Originally from Taipei, Shih-yu had been working as a designer when his passion for visual storytelling led him to the UK to study for a master's degree in illustration, thereby unleashing his hitherto shackled world of characters. Since graduating in 2017, he has been shortlisted for the Cheltenham Illustration Awards and the Golden Pinwheel Young Illustrators Competition, held as part of the China Shanghai International Children's Book Fair. Shih-yu's first author-illustrated book, *An Ordinary Story*, was published by Troika Books in the UK in the summer of 2018, and he has contributed illustrations to a number of other books and magazines, both in English and in Chinese.

'I enjoy drawing things to make people laugh and smile, just as was the case with my first admirer, my mom, whose smiles are still in my memory, encouraging me to keep on drawing. As for sketchbooks, basically I use them mainly in two ways: one is for projects and one is for observational drawings, to build up my memory drawing bank. Sketchbooks are always like an asylum, a place where I can experiment and play with anything in advance of getting to the finishing stages. I like to play around with characters in my sketchbooks, even in observational drawings. I find it quite useful as I find I can draw my characters much more naturally – especially their movements – in my finished projects.

'Over the last few years, I have done quite a lot of finished work with a digital device, but I found that the excitement and lovely accidents from the paper sketchbooks were difficult to replicate. So I still love to use sketchbooks for observational drawings and sometimes just for personal, fun projects –which are the most enjoyable part!'

opposite & pages 174–177
Shih-yu Lin's illustration practice is based on many years of drawing from direct observation in locations around the world. The drawings themselves demonstrate a keen interest in the relationship between people and their environments, and often in the light that falls on them. However, the urge to populate such drawings with the occasional passing comic character sometimes proves too difficult to resist.

Hauptbahnhof
1 December 2018

Shih-yu Lin

We should go there

Nicole had done
her first exam on
today. Hopefully it
will be a good
start.

Soho Park
27 October 2017

National Portrait Gallery
14 August 2018

Trafalgar Square
14 August 2018

Shih-yu Lin

Notting Hill
P 7 July 2018

Maritime Museum.

Shih-yu Lin

Sara Lundberg

Describing herself as a 'narrative artist', Sara Lundberg clearly prefers to avoid such labels as 'illustrator' or 'painter'. A winner of multiple awards, she has illustrated more than thirty children's books, many in her native Sweden, and has exhibited works at, among other places, Örebro Art Gallery, Gothenburg Museum of Art and Eskilstuna Art Museum. In 2013, she was one of a number of illustrators selected to represent Sweden for the duration of its tenure as guest country at that year's Bologna Children's Book Fair.

Lundberg's book *The Bird Within Me* was first published in Sweden in 2017, by Mirando Bok, and then in English, by Book Island, in 2020. After winning numerous awards in Sweden, it was shortlisted for the prestigious Kate Greenaway Medal in the UK. It is a story inspired by the letters and diaries of the Swedish expressionist painter Berta Hansson, who died in 1994. In an interview with Greet Pauwelijn, founder of Book Island, Lundberg explained the thrust of the book: 'It's about having the courage to follow your dream. Bertha wants to be an artist, she feels that from a very early age, but it's not accepted in the time in which she grows up and in the village where she's expected to do what others have done, being a girl – take care of the home, the animals and the children, and marry someone in the village. It's about having the courage to be different and figuring out who you want to be.'

The story is told primarily through images, with accompanying extracts from Hansson's diaries. The artworks, most of which fill double-page spreads, are mainly executed in fluid watercolour but sometimes incorporate more opaque media, including paint, pencil and collage. As she explained to the Picturebook Makers blog, 'In other illustrations I simplify, using collage and thick paint. Characters go towards the abstract. Broad strokes with the brush. Only expression. Here, the goal is imperfection, almost towards the ugly and unfinished. It was important for me to allow myself to be inconsistent. The characters didn't *have* to look the same on each spread, I didn't *have* to stick to a specific style or technique. So I just did each scene intuitively.'

Lundberg's observations are borne out by her sketchbooks. There is no attempt at stylistic trickery or facility; rather, every page is clearly driven by the pursuit of an idea or concept, or a simple urge to capture a moment as honestly and directly as possible.

'I started keeping a journal, or a sketchbook – for me it is the same thing – when I was eighteen. I was an exchange student in the US and happened to go to a high school with an extraordinary art department, which had an extraordinary art teacher. He strongly encouraged us to be very active with our sketchbooks. And at the end of the week, we had an open critique of them in the classroom. Since then, I always have a sketchbook handy. I carry it with me always. I feel naked without it. There can be long periods when I don't use it, but I still have it with me, just in case an idea pops up, or I see something that needs to be jotted down. It can be urgent when it comes.

'The sketchbook is just for me; it's not meant for showing to anybody. I mix writing with drawing. I test ideas. I sometimes draw what I see, and other times there are images from my imagination. I write down what I dream at night. Seeds to stories that pop up. My struggles. Inspiration. Goals. I have a whole bookshelf of sketchbooks in different colours, mostly black. Sometimes I go through them in search of something I have forgotten. I can open a sketchbook from 2002 and find an idea to a painting, or a poem or a story, that is still usable. Sometimes looking back can be a reminder of where I was, and where I am now.'

opposite & pages 180–182
Sara Lundberg's notebooks are filled with visual ideas for later projects, such as paintings or narratives, and quick, observational studies.

page 183
An unusually resolved image of boxers and audience from one of Lundberg's notebooks.

Sara Lundberg

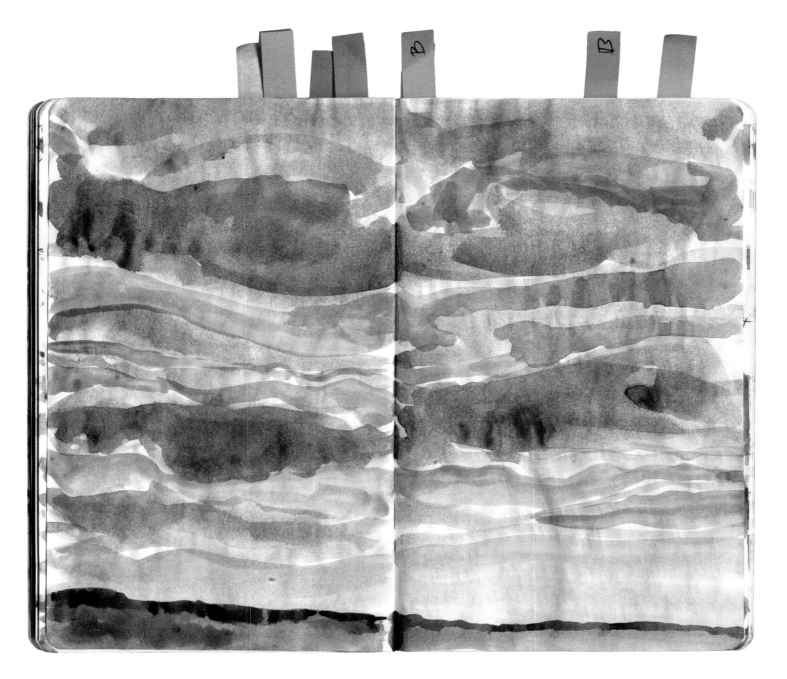

Sara Lundberg

EZ på stranden
Sommaren 2013

FILMER

- Donny Darko
- The dangerous life of the AlterBoys
- I'm not a serial killer

Omslag

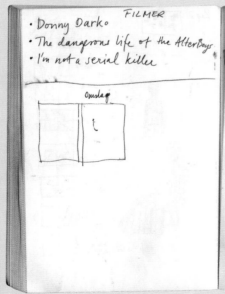

Idé till målning.

Den engelske rovdjursdressören Martin Lacey förekade inte
att gå i närkontakt med sina lejon.

med Ezra i och sjönk omedelbart.
Jag dök i och fick tag i honom
och simmade iland. Allt slutade
väl.

183

Manuel Marsol

Among the many awards bestowed on the acclaimed Spanish illustrator Manuel Marsol is the prestigious International Award for Illustration – BCBF/Fundación SM, which he received in 2017 for *La leyenda de don Fermín* ('The Legend of Don Fermín', Ediciones SM). His instantly recognizable, powerful and personal visual language has led to his books being published in numerous languages around the world. Marsol studied advertising and visual communication before working as an art director in advertising for three years. He clearly thinks deeply about his work, and his detailed analysis of the role of the sketchbook in his practice will undoubtedly strike a chord with many other illustrators.

'I think that one of the strengths of the notebook is its ability to downplay the work and lighten our excess of responsibility when drawing. We know that a good piece of loose paper can paralyse us, but the notebook allows itself to be tamed in a special way. A small emotional relationship is created with [the notebook] that can influence the drawing and encourages [you] to continue until it is completed, as if it were a collection or an album of stickers. Who does not feel the pleasure of holding a notebook overflowing with drawings, with wavy pages, through which time has passed? A lot of time is spent with some notebooks, sometimes months and years, and that generates an intimacy that a loose piece of paper or a digital file does not give you. It's like a friend you don't need to impress because he already knows you, and that allows you to act more freely. The personal notebook judges you less than any work you do with the intention of being finished or complete. And on many occasions, the final artworks come directly from there, because one starts them without the pressure of knowing that they will be the definitive ones.

Having the notebook with me gives me security, even if I don't always use it. There are illustrators who draw at all hours, on the bus, people in cafes, etc. There are others who don't, who can go several days without drawing. I am one of the latter. Sometimes I simply spend my time walking around with the notebook in my backpack, as if this would recharge its powers until I am ready to go back to it.

'When I conceive pages of a picturebook, book covers or posters, I usually draw very

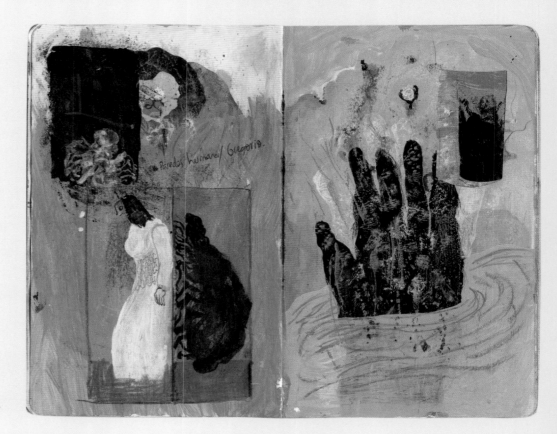

small in the notebook to get an overall idea of the composition. This allows me to quickly see if the image works or if it has balance, and it makes it easy for me to discard because it took me little effort and time to develop it. I do it with a pen and not with a pencil, so I force myself not to go around erasing and quickly jump from one option to another while maintaining a certain freshness. If I made big, elaborate sketches, I would lose that quick-trace grace and it would be more difficult for me to detach them, cross them out or correct them. That

opposite & right
Two spreads from one
of Marsol's sketchbooks
showing the development
of ideas for his illustrated
edition of Franz Kafka's
Metamorphosis (Astro
Rey, 2015).

Manuel Marsol

left
A third spread showing Marsol's ideas for his edition of Franz Kafka's *Metamorphosis*.

opposite
A personal project from one of Marsol's sketchbooks, executed while working at a creative residency in 2021 at Manoir de la Moissie in Périgord, France.

is why many times my notebooks are pages and pages of small rectangles barely the size of a thumb, of miniature pages, with multiple versions of an idea, with micro variations until they are distilled into a final composition.

'It is as if the thought were shaped and developed in that instant. Sometimes it's just a matter of persevering. Hover over a thought in a notebook and not inside the head. The notebook helps to establish and fix all those connections and intuitions that are part of the creative process, which in my case – and I think in the majority of those who are dedicated to this – is never a direct path. It's about hanging around, deviating without really knowing why. The path only becomes clear when it is finished. It is rather an accumulation that ends up falling under its own weight. In a way, it is as if the feeling of being lost in writing things down in the notebook, or wandering around [apparently getting] nowhere, were precisely the key for solutions to appear. Maybe they don't show up while you're writing or drawing; maybe they show up while you're having breakfast or taking a nap. But without that writing or drawing in the notebook, it's very difficult for them to jump out at you during your nap.

'That is why notebooks can also be an infinite trap. In some projects they have become for me authentic labyrinths with no exit, or with multiple valid exits, which is almost worse. One opens so many paths and so many possibilities in a notebook that it becomes very difficult to make decisions, discard and choose. There are projects that I would like to do without writing so much: quotes, readings, references to films or other artists that are related in some way to the project, style and aesthetic options, different conceptual approaches to the same work, etc. What is

known as "analysis paralysis". And at some point in the process one has to know how to close that notebook, decide and draw. If a project takes several years, sometimes I find that I have written down the same idea in two different notebooks. Something that I had forgotten and that suddenly seems very witty to me. And when I go back or open an old notebook, I realize that I had already been there. We are condemned to repeat ourselves; our artistic interests have their limits and what moves us we carry inside and it comes out again and again. It also happens that treasures buried years ago come out of notebooks. And you usually like them because you buried them. They are like a gift from someone who knows you very well.

'The notebook also helps me to remember the importance of feeling pleasure drawing, [which I sometimes] forget if I'm too busy trying to solve a project. Enjoying drawing seems obvious to an illustrator, but I know many illustrators, me the first, who suffer at certain points in their career because everything they draw seems to have a function or a goal. And although the notebook is the perfect medium to develop projects, it is also the perfect way to draw for drawing's sake. Drawing without knowing why, wasting time but actually appropriating it, without visual references and only with the imagination, just to stain the paper or to try a new material, without even being clear about what you are drawing – it seems to me essential [to] enjoying this profession. Drawing for drawing's sake has saved me on more than one occasion, and I'm not just talking professionally. The pleasure of drawing without direction opens unexpected paths, something essential to [maintaining] the ability to surprise oneself.'

Manuel Marsol

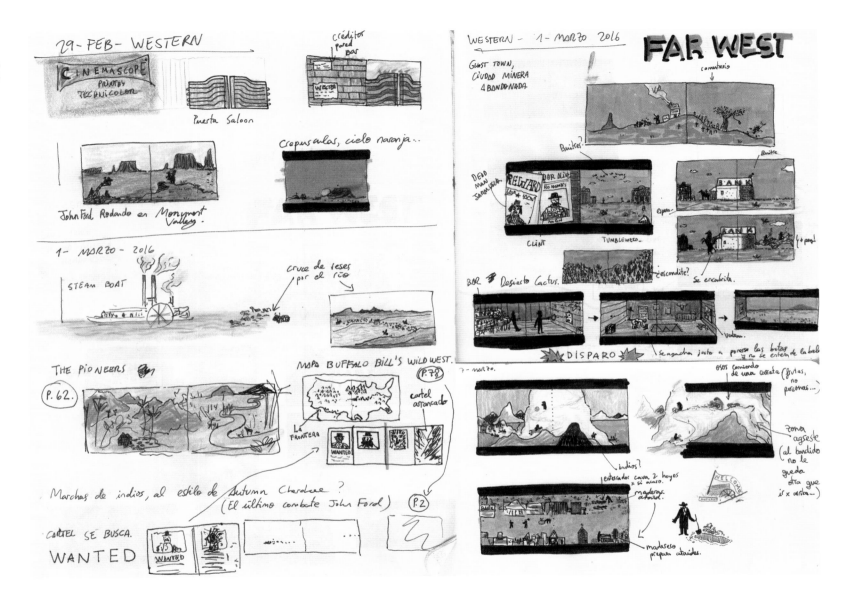

Manuel Marsol

An illustrator, printmaker and lecturer at Leeds Beckett University, Mick Marston says he has drawn for as long as he can remember, starting with cowboys, Indians, tanks, aeroplanes and footballers. Later, as a music fan, he was drawn to the covers of punk LPs, and to the idea of becoming a designer himself. He had not realized, however, that he would need to go to art college, so he left school at sixteen and worked as a screen printer in a graphics studio for six years. Although his interest in graphic design had been consolidated, he felt he was 'going nowhere' and decided to return to education. After completing his A levels and an art foundation course, he went on to study printmaking in Leeds.

Following his graduation, Marston exhibited some linocuts at Leeds City Gallery and was contacted by an art director, who commissioned him to provide illustrations for an advertising campaign. He had never seen himself as an illustrator, but was soon being represented by CIA (Central Illustration Agency) in London, working for a range of prestigious clients. His insatiable and eclectic visual appetite has resulted in a huge range of influences, but he reserves particular mention for Eduardo Paolozzi, Pablo Picasso, Saul Steinberg and Philip Guston.

'My work has gradually shifted over the years. It was quite linear to begin with; now it's more refined, more shape-based, but is open to subtle changes depending on the brief or the client.

'The sketchbooks have always been a major part of my practice, but up until recently were hidden. They have always been a place to work things out. I have no fear of drawing, even bad drawing. Some of the better shapes come from the worst drawings; it's the ability to recognize what makes a good shape or a bad shape, if that makes sense. They were always a place to put down ideas for later works too. I'd often go back to a sketchbook from ten years ago to see if something resonates now which didn't at the time.

'We had a staff exhibition at Leeds Beckett, as it was then called, entitled *Brains on Paper*, where staff showed the stuff they do before the end product to try to get students to value this process more, as opposed to delivering a fait accompli. I hung about twenty sketchbooks and changed the pages daily. Students loved it, so I did it again at an external one-man show and the public loved it too. I think maybe this demonstrates that making pictures is achievable; like seeing the wizard in *The Wizard of Oz*, it's not magic. "Brains on paper" is definitely what it is, though. I like to experiment with form and line and media – thin lines, thick lines, coloured lines, black lines, white lines, no lines, lots of lines, dotted lines, lines made with tape, straight lines drawn with a ruler, circles drawn with a template or a compass, no straight lines allowed, no curves allowed, painted lines, dribbled lines, lines to make things look more complex, lines which follow the squared paper. Flat forms, isometric, axonometric, bad perspective, collage made from old drawings or prints, coloured backgrounds, drawings over drawings over drawings, limited colour palettes, too many colours, using the wrong colours, blending, shading, pencils, pens, brushes, sticks, tape, etc.

'And then there's the content – what am I going to draw? Regular themes: cars, aeroplanes, shoes, guitars, architecture, tanks, animals, cartoon characters, trees, gardens and people. Usually related to current affairs or something I'm doing, or

opposite & pages 192–195
Mick Marston's sketchbooks clearly demonstrate a fascination with the geometric and with exploring the boundaries of readability in representational, pictorial terms.

Mick Marston

Illustrators' Sketchbooks

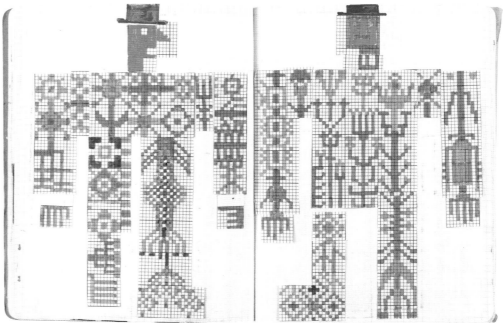

something related to lecturing. I rarely have a set idea in my head – I just let it come out. I'm quite interested in automatic drawing, but generally not pure abstraction. I like to push how far I can get away from an object or thing to see how it is still recognizable or at what point it becomes too abstracted to communicate. I like Picasso's guitar series from the 1910s; I think this demonstrates what I'm getting at. If I run out of space on the page, then the guitar neck can be at a right angle to the body – it's still a guitar. I'm also interested in what illustration can do when you think beyond what is only visible. A car full of people is incredibly complex. At one end of the spectrum, you have what amounts to a severed head inside a rectangle and

a square with two circles. At the other end, the car has reflections in the bodywork, different ones in the windows; it has mirrors and lights. If you have X-ray vision, it has an engine and fluid running around it, and upholstery and stuffing and air bags and a dashboard with numbers on. The people have features and clothes and flesh and bones and thoughts and speech; the car emits fumes and makes a noise ... Illustration can capture all that – it's just then a process of editing and composition.

'I suppose flatness has always been part of the stuff I like: logos, characters, packaging, etc. as a kid, then graphic stuff when I became a screen printer. It was never

a deliberate decision to not do perspective or realism; you just gravitate to something that works for you. I've been trying to think of ways to make use of the sketchbook work – to monetize it, basically; I need to eat. The linocut version of the car image is the most successful in translating my own hand to a process that can be repeated. The refinement process for my illustration work takes away my own hand somewhat due to the nature of translating the drawing in Illustrator. I suppose I'm not comfortable selling the unadulterated drawing. I never deliberately make a drawing to sell or exhibit; they are means to a different end. I think something would be lost if I thought too much about it.'

Illustrators' Sketchbooks

Bernd Mölck-Tassel

Born in 1964, in the northern German state of Schleswig-Holstein, Bernd Mölck-Tassel lives in the countryside in a small village to the north of Hamburg. He originally studied illustration at the Hamburg University of Applied Sciences, where he is now a professor of book illustration and the head of the illustration department. While still a student at the university in the late 1980s, he was already undertaking editorial commissions for leading magazines and newspapers – something he continues to do alongside his award-winning work as an illustrator and maker of picturebooks, collaborating with such writers as Dieter Böge. As an artist-academic, he thinks deeply about the role of the sketchbook in relation to his own practice:

'In my illustration studies, I was constantly drawing in sketchbooks. I spent more time with these sketchbooks than on the "official" assignments of the courses. My goal was always to become a good draughtsman. I noted down the shapes and compositions of the forms of the visible world in the sketchbook to get closer to this goal. In doing so, I did not realize that I was learning more than I was aware of. I casually sensitized myself to abstraction, composition, rhythm, light and shadow, dynamics and stillness, compression and opening, perspective, spatiality and anatomy. I learned to concentrate extremely well over a long period of time. I loved being outside and exploring a landscape or a city, walking and drawing.

'Then, when I started to become a professional illustrator, I hardly kept sketchbooks, but developed ideas in the studio on individual papers. I tried to create interesting and challenging text–image relationships.

'At some point I started drawing in the sketchbook again. But something had changed. Instead of observing and analysing the visual appearance of the outer world, as I had done before, I began to draw my inner ideas and thoughts. I created my own world. Instead of absorbing the outer world into myself, I extracted my inner world outwards.

'When I was commissioned to create illustrations for [Franz Schubert's song cycle] *Winterreise* for the [German newspaper] *Frankfurter Allgemeine Sonntagszeitung*, I spent weeks in my studio unsuccessfully searching for an idea to illustrate Schubert's twenty-four songs. Frustrated, I travelled to the book fair in Bologna. On the terrace of a cafe, sketching in my sketchbook, something flowed from my pen that surprised me. I had found the right approach, the central guideline, the visual sound for the project.

'In the sketchbook, I like to work intuitively/associatively on series of images and ever-new variations on the same theme. Sketching is a way of getting in touch with my subconscious. It helps me to think without words. In the process, as with automatic writing in literature, I come up with solutions that surprise me. It's as if I were digging for gold and suddenly hit a vein. Or as if my sailing ship, after days in the doldrums, were to turn into a sudden wind and finally pick up speed again.

'With the sketchbook, I can take my studio with me on my trips and journeys around the world. A "studio for the pocket".'

right & pages 198–199
Examples of Bernd
Mölck-Tassel's sketchbook
studies for a commission
to illustrate Franz
Schubert's *Winterreise*
song cycle for the
German newspaper
*Frankfurter Allgemeine
Sonntagszeitung.*

197

Illustrators' Sketchbooks

Bernd Mölck-Tassel

left
A spread from one of
Bernd Mölck–Tassel's
sketchbooks from his days
as a student in the 1980s.

opposite
Sketchbook ideas for
'*Und Was Sagt Mama?*'
('And What Does Mama
Say?'), a book project
with the writer Dieter
Böge. Mölk–Tassel usually
photographs the slightly
coloured drawings with his
iPad and then develops
them further in Procreate.

Bernd Mölck-Tassel

Ed Merlin Murray

A graduate of the University of Cumbria in Carlisle, Ed Merlin Murray has made a name for himself in the world of music, creating album covers, videos and publicity material for a range of international artists. His entrepreneurial activities extend into printmaking and selling both lino and screen prints. His sketchbooks and personal work, he says, tend to deal with issues of the mind, and especially mental health.

'Sketchbooks are a crucial part of my overall practice. All of my personal work begins in a sketchbook, whether the final piece is drawing, painting or 3D digital animation. My sketchbook is where I check in with my technical skills while experimenting in a low-pressure environment – there are no "mistakes" in a sketchbook because I set myself no standards. The work in there isn't necessarily for sharing with others, although sometimes I do so if a page or spread turns out to be in some way pleasing. For every bit I do share, though, there are nine others that will remain forever hidden away.

'Unless the brief specifies otherwise, I try to take elements from my current sketchbook work into whatever commissioned work I'm doing. This might be something as simple as the use of my current favourite drawing tools, or as abstract as taking elements of composition, shape, colour or theme and applying them to the job. My sketchbook is also where I try to define whatever my current "style" is – something that is always gently changing.

'The general idea when working in my sketchbook is simply to play. I realized a while ago that play is very important if I want to make interesting, engaging work. If I simply move from commercial project to commercial project, my work quickly becomes staid, boring and unadventurous. I don't tend to use sketchbooks for project-based work; all of my sketches for these are done on A3 layout paper, enabling me to keep everything connected to a project in the same folder. Despite this, each book seems to have a theme, even if just reflecting the things that I was thinking about or looking at at the time.

'I usually have several sketchbooks on the go at once. I leave them all over my house and studio and work in them all concurrently. My favourites at the moment are made by Magma and are quite big and thick, with paper which is at once fairly heavy and textured, and also unexpectedly transparent. I like to photograph these on a lightbox, before colouring the resulting image digitally, incorporating both the linework on the page in question and whatever is bleeding through from the reverse.

'I'm a bit of a recluse, so a lot of the drawings in my sketchbooks are made from photographs. It's either that or my own face, which has become boring to draw ... Whenever I do venture out, I tend to have a pair of little Muji sketchbooks in different sizes on me – the ones with the flimsy, off-white paper – and I love to make very quick drawings in ink or graphite of the people around me. These books are also the ones in which I scribble ideas for future drawings, little comics or bits of animation.'

opposite & pages 204–205
Whether directly or indirectly, much of Ed Merlin Murray's personal sketchbook work focuses on issues relating to the mind: mental health, neuroscience, bipolarity.

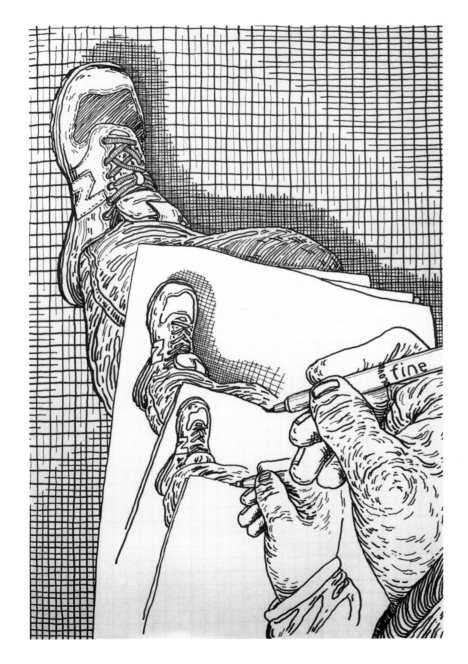

Ed Merlin Murray

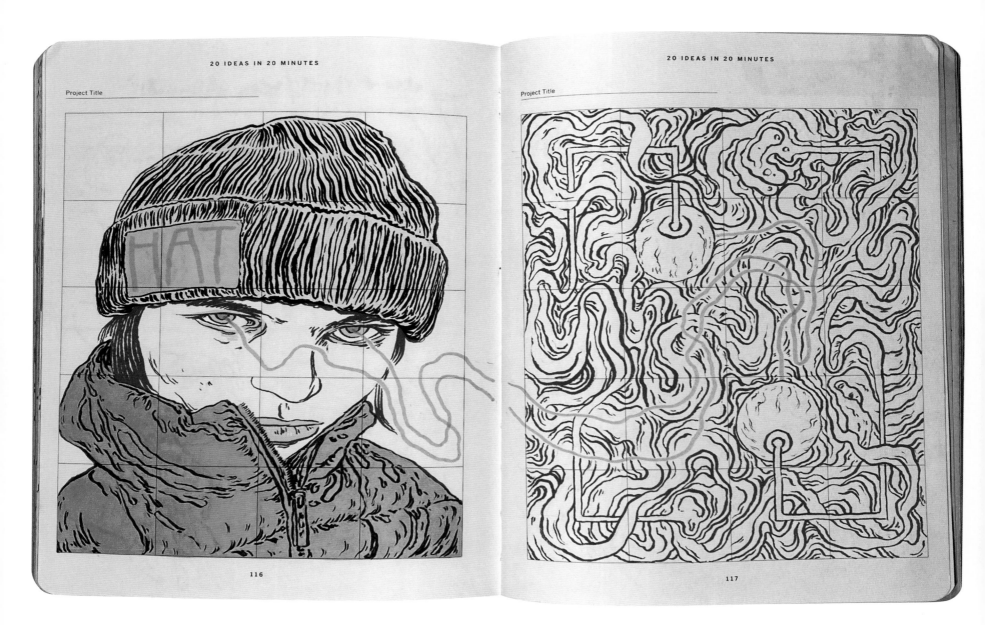

Project Title

Project Title

Fabian Negrin

Originally from Córdoba, Argentina, Negrin is now an Italian citizen based in Milan. After studying graphic design, illustration and painting at the Metropolitan Autonomous University in Mexico City, Negrin undertook a master's degree at the Academy of Fine Arts San Carlos. His prolific output as an award-winning illustrator and picturebook-maker is notable not only for its exceptional technical quality but also for its restless experimentation with wide-ranging visual languages. Running throughout his work is a sense of dream-like otherworldliness. His picturebooks and illustrated books, both those written by himself and those made in collaboration with writers past and present, have been published in multiple languages around the world.

Negrin's sketchbooks are surprising in many ways. His intricately rendered finished paintings stand in dramatic contrast to the direct, childlike, almost crude drawings in the sketchbooks. It is as if he is trying to catch a visual idea before it escapes – with urgency, and unencumbed by technique.

'I don't go around with a sketchbook. I should, as I think it would be profitable, but I don't. I only do this when I go on holiday, but I end up doing only a couple of observational drawings of the place and then I use it for other purposes. And these purposes are the same for which I use the sketchbooks in my studio ... I often use them there, at home. The use I make of them is basically jotting down ideas, ideas for stories, visual ideas, puns, or transcribing phrases from books I've read or thoughts that have come to me

about illustration, art, etc. In this last case the writing serves to focus the thought, to make it become more crystalline. In the case of visual ideas, however, it is always a rough and graceless type of drawing. It comes to me like this; I wish it were more beautiful, but looking at the sketchbooks the little attention paid to the line is, unfortunately, evident. It's the opposite of what I do in my finished artwork, I'd say. Often these are things that come out in parallel to the books I'm working on.

'The many sketches for the books I make are always made on loose sheets of paper, not in sketchbooks – and I always throw away my sketches. Consequently, in the sketchbooks there is very little trace of my published books. Sometimes the initial idea remains. This remains because it usually came to me while I was doing another book. I leave it in there and maybe one day it becomes a book too. The majority do not. Many of these drawings and thoughts, then, go beyond my work as an author and illustrator of children's books. They are often obscene, as if the sketchbook were there to allow me to annotate things that I know I will most likely not publish but that interest me. A kind of diary of the unconscious, perhaps. Essentially, they are a series of naked and raw ideas, with no element that can give them more strength than they potentially have in themselves. Obviously, every idea is born small, and there is always the risk of not considering its possible virtues, of killing it before it can walk on its own feet. In this sense, sketchbooks are a kind of incubator that keeps very fragile babies alive, sometimes indefinitely, never to leave the incubator.'

below
One of Fabian Negrin's sketchbooks, complete with an illustration on the cover.

opposite
A pencil study after a work by the Sicilian-born Art Nouveau illustrator and poster designer Aleardo Terzi. Negrin has a keen interest in the history of illustration and illustrators.

this page & opposite
Fabian Negrin's roughly
drawn initial sketches
often contrast starkly with
the intensity of technique
used in rendering the final,
published illustrations, as
seen here in a page from
his book *Come? Cosa?*
('As? What?', Orecchio
Acerbo, 2016; opposite).
Also in evidence are
the visual ideas and
word puns that feature
frequently in Negrin's
sketchbooks.

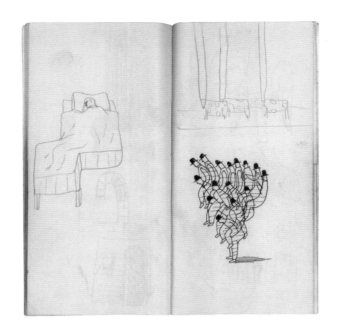

IL MARINAIO CHIEDE ALLA SUA MOGLIE
DI PREPARARLE PER CENA UNA
DETERMINATA COSA (DICIAMO LENTICCHIE)
MA LA BREZZA DISTORCE LE SUE PAROLE
E LEI CAPISCE UN'ALTRA COSA (CHE FA
RIMA CON LENTICCHIE).

Fabian Negrin

Beatrix Potter

In 2022, an exhibition at the Victoria and Albert Museum in London, *Beatrix Potter: Drawn to Nature*, confirmed not only Potter's general popularity but also her international cultural significance. The exhibition, coming almost 120 years after the publication of Potter's first books, offered visitors a chance to see beyond the well-known and well-loved characters and into the world of intense observation that led to their creation – a world of landscape and

natural-history studies, including detailed renderings of botanical and zoological subjects. Much of this took place in her sketchbooks, which have helped to enlarge our understanding of the artist and the books that have sold more than 250 million copies worldwide.

Growing up in south-west London, Potter was familiar with both the V&A (or the South

Kensington Museum, as it was then known)
and the nearby Natural History Museum,
visiting them regularly to draw. She also had
an unusual collection of pets: rabbits, mice,
lizards, frogs, ducks, snails and insects.
These too she would draw, alive or dead, in
an unsentimental, analytical way. Some, such
as the mice, would of necessity be drawn very
quickly, multiple times across a sheet of paper
in order to capture movement and posture.

Potter's careful approach to drawing began
in childhood, the earliest sketchbook in the
V&A's collection having been executed when
she was just eight years old, on a family
holiday to Scotland. Crudely made by hand
from folded sheets of writing paper, some
bearing the letterhead 'Bolton Gardens,
South Kensington', the sketchbook is labelled
'Dalguise, Dunkeld, Perthshire', where the
family regularly stayed in the summer. There
are sketches in pencil, sometimes coloured
with watercolour washes – a combination
of media that she would continue to use in
adulthood – of insects, birds' eggs, butterflies,
moths, wildflowers and landscapes.
The drawings are accompanied by pencil
notes, some of them left unfinished. One
page of studies of caterpillars on leaves is
exceptionally accomplished for a child so
young. Her fascination with the natural
world was already firmly established.

In 1905, Potter bought Hill Top, a working
farm near Sawrey, a village in the Lake
District she had fallen in love with on
previous visits. It is believed that the plan
had been to buy the farm with Norman
Warne, to whom she had become engaged.
Warne, however, died that year of pernicious
anaemia. Potter decided to go ahead
with the purchase, and many of her books
were created at Hill Top in the decade after
Warne's death.

**opposite, below &
pages 212–213**
Beatrix Potter's love of
the Lake District is evident
in the many sketchbook
studies that she made
of the changing seasons
and light.

Beatrix Potter

Beatrix Potter

Eric Ravilious

The large volume of work produced by Eric Ravilious during his tragically short life has come to be appreciated – for its originality and sensitivity – alongside the work of his friend Edward Bawden and that of a number of other mid-century British artist-illustrator-designers. The 2022 film about Ravilious's life, *Drawn to War*, has generated further interest not only in this artist's highly recognizable output, across painting, illustration, printmaking and design, but also in his death in 1942 off the coast of Iceland while serving as an official war artist. The plane in which he was travelling failed to return from an expedition to search for another missing aircraft. Ravilious's ability to capture in watercolour the sharp light of his native South Downs, often while painting directly into the sun, was perfectly expressed by the author and painter Olive Cook, writing in 1988 in the original catalogue of the Fry Art Gallery in Saffron Walden, Essex: 'Early familiarity with the landscape of the Sussex Downs, vast and mysterious, gently billowing, chalk-pale and luminous, with the sea below them, determined the abiding character of his art, its radiance and remoteness.'

left, opposite & pages 216–217
Eric Ravilious's 1936 scrapbook was assembled 'in one go' from various other, more eclectic collections in order to focus on preliminary drawings for illustrations and paintings. It includes studies for such watercolours as *Newhaven Harbour* (opposite left) and *Channel Steamer Leaving Harbour* (opposite right), costume designs, and tonal studies for wood engravings.

Eric Ravilious

For a short while in the 1930s, having met and studied together at the Royal College of Art in the previous decade, Ravilious and Bawden shared a house in the Essex village of Great Bardfield with their artist wives, Tirzah Garwood and Charlotte Epton. They were both forging reputations as illustrators through their wide-ranging work for print and ceramic design. Ravilious was particularly adept at wood engraving, a medium that had enjoyed a revival in the 1920s and which he would continue to use throughout his career, for book illustration, advertising, decorative motifs and book plates. Bawden felt that the wood engravings were key to his friend's visual vocabulary, and that, for Ravilious, the process of cutting into the block *was* the drawing. In 1972, Bawden recalled

that, 'Like Thomas Bewick, [Ravilious] was a white line engraver. On the block the design was not drawn in line or black ink, but merely as a shaded pencil drawing that served only as a guide for the real drawing that was done by the graver in the act of cutting into the surface of the boxwood. Thus it is that Eric's engravings have a freedom, liveliness and invention that has not been equalled since the days of Bewick.'

As with many of his illustrator and designer contemporaries, Ravilious kept what are probably best described as scrapbooks, rather than sketchbooks. Yet they are predominantly filled with pencil drawings and designs that have been cut from other books or sheets of paper. The spreads reproduced

here are from the scrapbook held at the Fry Art Gallery. It was actually constructed as a single work by Ravilious in 1936 during a process of 'culling' much of the work that had been in several other ongoing scrapbooks, removing the general collected ephemera and work of other artists and retaining his own working drawings and designs.

Sheila Robinson

One of a group of English artists who came to live in a small village in rural Essex, Sheila Robinson worked across a wide range of graphic-arts disciplines, including illustration for books, magazines and advertising, printmaking for exhibition, and even the design of animal characters for fairground rides at Blackpool Pleasure Beach. The village in Essex was Great Bardfield, and the artists who settled their included Edward Bawden, Eric Ravilious, Michael Rothenstein, Kenneth Rowntree and the textile designer Marian Straub.

Born in Nottinghamshire in 1925, Robinson studied at Nottingham School of Art. After a brief period in the Women's Land Army during the Second World War, she was taught by Bawden at the Royal College of Art. Along with some of her fellow RCA students, she would later assist Bawden with his mural work for the 1951 Festival of Britain on London's South Bank. The two remained lifelong friends.

The artist Chloë Cheese, one of Robinson's two children, remembers her mother working on the kitchen table of their cottage late into the evening. After she became divorced from her children's father – another of the Bardfield artists, Bernard Cheese – Robinson needed to take on as many commissions as she could. Her regular clients included BBC Publications, for which she contributed illustrations for *The BBC Book of the Countryside* (1964); she also produced work for the *About Britain* guidebooks published by the Festival of Britain Office in the early 1950s, and for such educational booklets as *Time and Tune* and *Singing Together: Rhythm & Melody*. The latter were published in vast numbers, beautifully illustrated throughout, and enjoyed by millions of children during the 1950s and 1960s.

As a printmaker, Robinson worked with a range of processes but was particularly known for card-printing, a rarely used technique involving blocks of soft cardboard. It required the printmaker to cut away the areas not to be printed, as with linocuts, and then treat the remaining cardboard with PVA glue before rolling it with ink; the resulting prints were slightly more textured than those produced with linocuts. Robinson used this process for one of her best-known projects, illustrations for a lavish edition of D. H. Lawrence's *Sons and Lovers* published by the Limited Editions Club in 1975. In later life, Robinson taught at the Royal College of Art and is remembered by generations of students for her supportive presence.

The images shown here are from a sketchbook that Robinson completed as a student in the late 1940s. Held at the Fry Art Gallery in Saffron Walden, Essex, it contains a rich mix of observational drawing, costume research (carried out at the Victoria and Albert Museum), portrait studies and imaginative illustration.

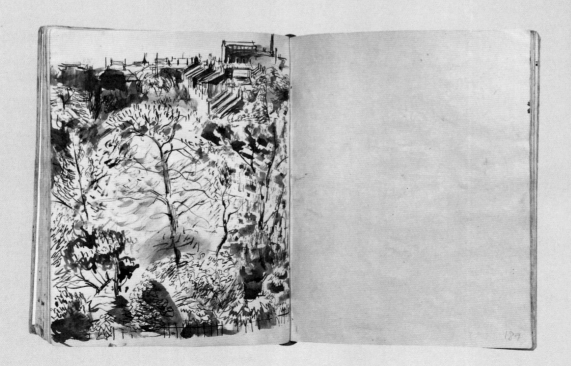

left & opposite
Two location-based observational studies. The double-page colour sketch is thought to be of Nottingham Goose Fair.

Goose Fair 45.

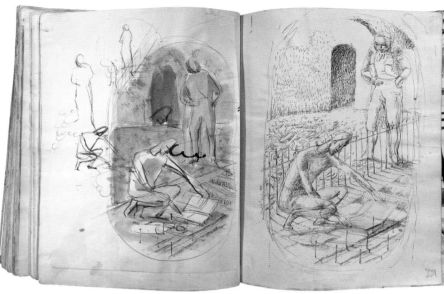

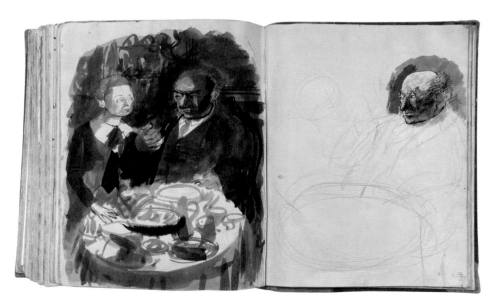

opposite
Studies and more finished work for unknown, imaginative student illustration projects.

above & right
Two portrait studies made from observation.

Sheila Robinson

Martin Salisbury

As a student in the 1970s, first at Cambridge School of Art and then at Maidstone College of Art, the importance of the sketchbook as a permanent companion was drummed into me by my tutors, in particular the painter John Bolam at Cambridge and then, at Maidstone, the Kate Greenaway Medal-winning children's book illustrator Gerald Rose. However, like many of my fellow illustrators, once I began working on a freelance basis, with the constant pressure of deadlines, the sketchbook was increasingly left to languish on a shelf, looking at me accusingly, or in a drawer. And as I became more involved with teaching illustration, another set of pressures (or perhaps excuses) took over. So my sketchbooks have been used primarily for life drawing, travel, allotments (something of an obsession) and occasional general anecdotal drawing, the last of these in pubs, cafes, markets, town centres or wherever *people* congregate.

It's a bit of a cliché to say that drawing people is important, but nothing can replace the kind of knowledge that can be gained from studying and trying to make visual sense of real live human beings, with all their myriad idiosyncrasies of behaviour and movement. In the life-drawing studio, I always seem to be at least as interested in observing the drawers as in studying the model – the intense concentration on their faces, the complete lack of awareness that they are being watched as all eyes (except mine) are glued to the model.

I like drawing in sketchbooks. In fact, like several other artists, I feel that many of my favourite pieces of work are to be found there. They are private, intimate. But there is always a danger that intimacy can tip over into preciousness, so it's important to make bad drawings freely (something that, to me at least, comes quite easily). I sometimes make my own sketchbooks, using my rudimentary bookbinding skills and some nice pattern papers – a job lot of which I bought a long time ago from an elderly bookbinder – for the boards.

The sketchbooks that are most important to me are the ones I filled many years ago on a number of two-week family holidays to an island in the Adriatic. I was obsessed with drawing and painting, getting out early every morning before the heat made it too uncomfortable and working as fast as possible to try to capture the intense feeling of being in that place, a place to which I had a strong connection. As the great mid-twentieth-century illustrator and painter John Minton said in a lecture at the City of Birmingham School of Printing in 1952, 'It's something to do with having a real love for the subject, having a real anxiety that it will escape: not just tolerating it as a possible subject, but loving it.' It's a sentiment I identify with very closely. When I dig out those holiday sketchbooks now, many years later, I find myself looking at each mark made and being transported back to that place and time, the smells, the heat, the sounds – all retained and buried away but released again as I turn the pages.

opposite
During two-hour life-drawing classes, I would often focus on the people drawing rather than the subject of their attention, the model. In this instance, I decided to spend the full two hours on a single ink-and-wash study.

Illustrators' Sketchbooks

right & opposite
A selection of spreads
from the sketchbooks
I filled during family
holidays to the Croatian
island of Šipan, using ink,
watercolour and gouache.

Martin Salisbury

Illustrators' Sketchbooks

above
Another spread from one
of my Šipan sketchbooks.

opposite
A quick ink-and-gouache
study made in the Spanish
city of Seville.

Seville - Sept 2003

Martin Salisbury

Ronald Searle

Cambridge School of Art it was drummed into us that we should not move, eat, drink or sleep without a sketchbook in the hand. Consequently, the habit of looking and drawing became as natural as breathing.'

After spending the early years of the war on manoeuvres in Norfolk and Scotland, Searle was put on a ship to Singapore, arriving just as it was falling to the Japanese. His incarceration for the remainder of the war in the notorious Changi Prison, including being forced to work on the Burma Railway, has been well documented. Yet throughout those years of starvation and disease, he continued to draw, using tiny scraps of paper that were begged or stolen and bound into sketchbooks. Speaking to me at his home in France in 2007, Searle said: '[S]o I thought, well, what I must do is appoint myself "unofficial" war artist and somehow make a record of what really happened in those years in case by any chance I managed to live and get out of it.' Had his sketchbooks been discovered by the camp guards, he would undoubtedly have been executed. But he hid them under the emaciated bodies of those of his fellow inmates who were suffering from cholera, knowing that his guards would never go near them for fear of being infected. Searle, who was one of the few who survived the camp, managed to bring his sketchbooks home. Today, many are held at the Imperial War Museum, London.

In the decades that followed his liberation, Searle became one of the most prolific and celebrated illustrators of his time. There were fewer opportunities to work in sketchbooks, but, alongside his work for books, magazines and advertising, he continued to practise reportage drawing through such projects as *Paris Sketchbook* (1950) and *Looking at London* (1953) – both of which he produced

with his wife, Kaye Webb – and, later, *Secret Sketchbook* (1970), the result of a commission from an American magazine to spend a week drawing in the notorious red light district of Hamburg.

After his death in 2011, I was invited by his family to return to Searle's home and bring back to the UK some items from his studio that related to his time at Cambridge School of Art, and which would be of interest to students. These included the sketchbooks/notebooks he used in later life – mostly for experimenting with tools and media – and various roughs, drawings and notes for personal projects, such as a memoir of his childhood in Cambridge and a wordless book titled 'The Hand', a satire on dictatorship and war.

For the nineteen-year-old Ronald Searle, the sketchbook would become something much more than a place to capture the everyday observations, thoughts and notes of an enthusiastic young art student. After barely a year as a full-time scholarship student at Cambridge School of Art, the outbreak of the Second World War dramatically altered his plans. His idyllic year as a student ('Lautrec was more precocious but he was never as happy as I was then', he later mused) was cut short when he was called up to serve in the Royal Engineers. Nevertheless, Searle was determined to continue to act on the advice of his art-school tutors. As he recalled in an interview with the UK-based Association of Illustrators several decades later, 'At the

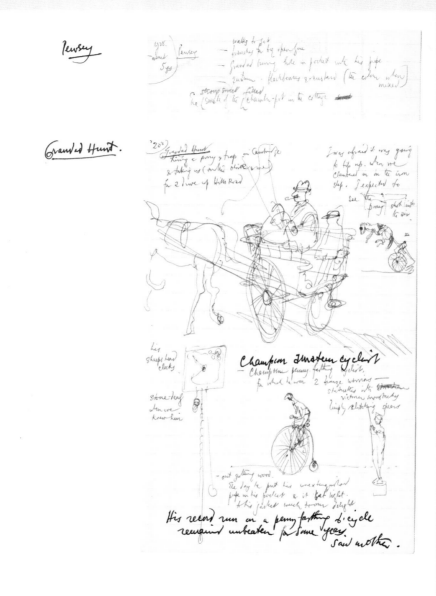

right & opposite
Ink and collage roughs
from Ronald Searle's
developmental notebook
for 'The Hand', an
unpublished, 'silent'
(or wordless) book.

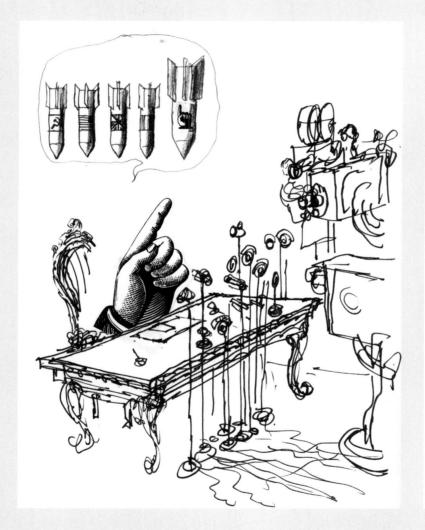

Ronald Searle

right
In a sketchbook titled 'Working Notes', Ronald Searle's fascination with and respect for his materials is evidenced by the pages of non-pictorial experiments devoted entirely to the exploration of the properties of particular inks and nibs.

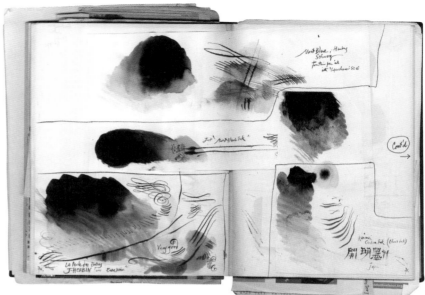

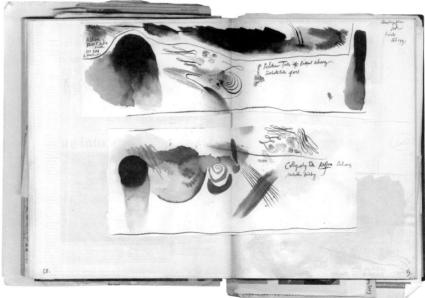

Illustrators' Sketchbooks

Ronald Searle

An award-winning illustrator and practice-based researcher, the Galicia-born artist and academic Beatriz Lostalé Seijo has worked for a wide range of clients, including V&A Publishing, Bloomsbury and various magazines and design periodicals. Her commissions have included designs for ceramic ware and fabrics, as well as traditional print. Here she discusses the use of her sketchbooks as research tools:

'Sketchbooks are a vital part of my practice. They allow me to explore, plan and reflect on the different processes I engage with when illustrating. I often use them in a non-linear way, going back and forth to include any relevant thoughts or drawings during both the creation process and in hindsight, creating a comprehensive record of raw ideas and images.

'The interest I have in non-fiction illustration has helped me to develop my sketchbooks to serve two purposes: the development of my personal ideas and the collection of factual information. While working on my projects it has become clear to me that I struggle to visualize images in advance. This is something that sketchbooks have helped to counteract by allowing me to progressively build the illustrations before me. Through their use, I can obtain a better insight into the individual components of the image, the compositions, and the look and feel of the finished product before working on the final artwork. When researching a non-fiction topic, however, the sketchbook becomes a place to filter, select and collect the relevant elements and data, while also acting as a means to analyse and understand through my practice the subject I am representing. The different rhythms of these processes are visible on the page, with the development of ideas involving more note-taking and a freer use of space, compared with a more organized approach when researching information.'

right, opposite & pages 236–237
Beatriz Lostalé Seijo's research and development sketchbooks are filled with imaginative yet highly methodical experimentation as she examines the potential for creative expression within the context of non-fiction illustration for children.

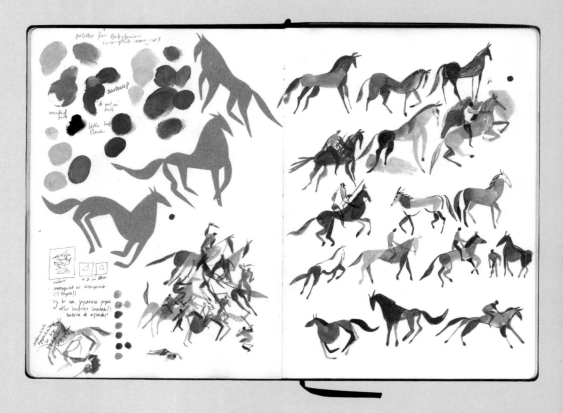

mashar. tz + anten cober ca
estaciones? + aban filos

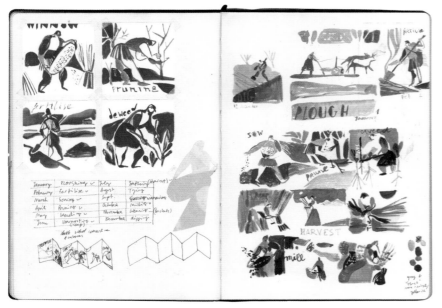

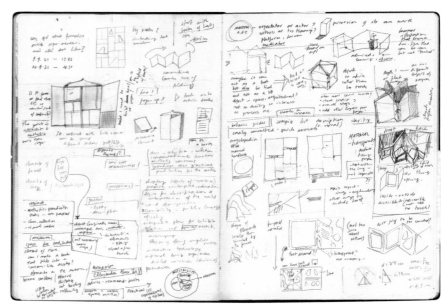

Beatriz Lostalé Seijo

Ana Sender

Born in Terrassa, Catalonia, Ana Sender studied painting and illustration at Massana art school in nearby Barcelona. Like many illustration graduates, she took on part-time jobs to support herself while working on her portfolio and trying to build a career as a freelance illustrator. As she puts it, 'I have never stopped drawing or imagining stories.' Gradually, she began to receive commissions for newspapers, magazines and books, as well as such fashion companies as the Madrid-based La Casita de Wendy, for which she was asked to produce pattern designs.

Today, Sender's picturebook work, as both maker and illustrator, is widely admired and can be appreciated in a growing number of languages. Whether she is working in fiction or non-fiction, there is a lyrical, dream-like quality to Sender's images. Indeed, dreams, she says, are an important influence on her work, together with the natural world and surrealism, fantasy and folk tales. These interests and influences can be seen in such publications as *The Cottingley Fairies* (NorthSouth Books, 2019), which she wrote and illustrated, and *Why Do We Cry?* (Kids Can Press, 2020), a collaboration with the writer Fran Pintadera. She claims to be, 'like most illustrators, more than a little chaotic'.

'I find it impossible to leave the house without a sketchbook and some pencils in my bag. Most of the time I won't even find the time to use it, but I need to know it's there, like a door or an ACME hole through which I can escape reality for a while. Some of my favourite places to draw in my sketchbooks are trains, cafes and bars. I love to create a bubble for myself while life happens around me.

'I have dozens of sketchbooks. Some of them contain stories or look like art objects, but most of them are chaotic, dirty, with ripped pages, ugly or unfinished drawings. I also have many sketchbooks where there are only one or two used pages and then they are abandoned because I felt it wasn't the right one at that moment.

'For sketching my professional projects, I prefer to use loose papers so I can arrange them all on the table, play with the order of the story and have a broader vision of the project. I prefer to use the sketchbooks to play, to experiment, to jump into the void. Of course, all of this is also reflected in my professional projects.'

below, opposite & pages 240–241
Ana Sender's sketchbooks are used for many different purposes. She says of this selection, 'I've tried to include diversity in the sketches, different techniques, some which are more like a finished illustration and other pages which are a bunch of small, unconnected sketches.'

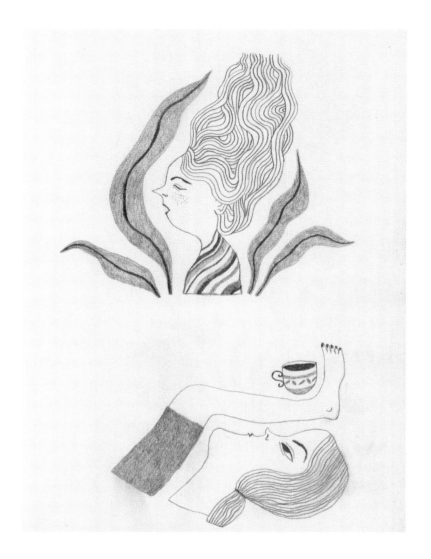

Ana Sender

Charles Shearer

For Charles Shearer, the sketchbook is the cornerstone of his practice as a printmaker, painter and teacher. He was born and brought up in Kirkwall, the largest town in the Orkney Islands, to the north of mainland Scotland. After leaving school, he headed to Aberdeen to study at Gray's School of Art, where he was taught by, among others, the illustrator, typographer and book designer George Mackie. He then headed to London, to study illustration at postgraduate level at the Royal College of Art, and has remained close to the college in west London ever since.

On the bookshelves of Shearer's Fulham home, alongside his collection of illustrated books and books about illustration, painting and printmaking, is a long, neat row of his own sketchbooks, the majority being small (210 × 130-mm/8 × 5-in.) Moleskines. Unnumbered and undated, they stretch back over the last few decades and are filled with observational studies, often reflecting his primary interest in landscape. But there are also many sequences of figure groups and several based on regular trips to London Zoo, as well as development studies for prints and paintings. The colour and tonal work reveals a printmaker's eye – complex scenes instinctively simplified into limited layers of shape, pattern and texture.

As a visiting teacher at art schools all around the United Kingdom, Shearer has inspired generations of illustration students to keep sketchbooks and to explore a range of printmaking techniques and processes as part of their education. He is particularly renowned for keeping alive the process of card-printing, something he learned from one of his tutors at the RCA, Sheila Robinson.

Most summers, Shearer takes himself off to Ireland, touring the countryside in search of derelict country houses, mansions and castles – subjects that appear in much of his print work, often punctuated by such contemporary features as pylons, telegraph poles, cars and boats. The Neo-Romantic nature of Shearer's art naturally lends itself to the illustration of poetry, and he is often associated with the work of George Mackay Brown, a fellow Orcadian.

'I have carried a notebook/sketchbook with me since I went to art school in 1975 ... They have developed over those years and have become, I guess, a record of my every day, as I plan and record what I am doing or where I am going, timetables and routes, where I am or what I am looking at. I currently keep a stock of A5 Ryman sketchbooks as I like the look and feel of them – the black covers, the soft, off-white paper with rounded corners. I realize I am now very particular about how this book feels, but at the same time not at all precious about how it is used ... They have become so familiar.

'I regularly take my sketchbook to London Zoo. To me, these visits form a kind of therapy as I engage with animals and exotic birds and spend time observing them. Not necessarily with any purpose in mind, but the pure enjoyment in responding to nature. The sketchbook is also a little thinking laboratory where an idea can be worked through, turned over perhaps in a series of brief thumbnails before I begin a piece of work or a print. Mostly just working out a composition ... I also carry a few pens, brush pens and pencils along with a craft knife in a handy clear pencil case. This is the minimum kit that travels everywhere with me.'

**opposite &
pages 244–245**
A selection of spreads from Charles Shearer's numerous sketchbooks.

Charles Shearer

/ mile End Park

245

Charles Shearer

Pam Smy

The divisions between sketchbook work and 'finished' illustration are mentioned repeatedly by many of the illustrators featured in this book. The issue of retaining the life and vigour of the sketchbook, escaping the clutches of the 'fear of finish' syndrome, rears its ugly head over and over again. Pam Smy, an author-illustrator, book-maker and pictorial novelist, is no exception. Although her beautiful sketchbooks are well known and widely admired, the difficulty in making the leap from sketchbook to imaginative illustration became, for Smy, something of a millstone around her neck. Her work as an illustration undergraduate had been very much observation-led and, indeed, sketchbook-led.

Recalling those undergraduate days in a 2017 interview with *Words & Pictures*, the online magazine of the Society of Children's Book Writers & Illustrators, Smy explained: 'Observational drawing became my obsession and I spent most of my three years drawing in working men's clubs, in pubs, at ballroom dance classes and in Women's Institute meetings. I loved it. But I graduated with a portfolio that was so based in the fact of what I had seen/could see that I had no skill in developing an imaginative voice. To explore the various ways that observation can feed into imaginative work has been my quest over the last twenty years.'

Later in the same interview, Smy described a commission to illustrate the children's novel *Lob* by Linda Newbery (David Fickling Books, 2010) as a key breakthrough. Newbery's story is set in a world that resonated with the themes that Smy was then exploring in her sketchbooks through observation; as a result, she found that she was able to more naturally combine direct observation with atmosphere and imagination. 'Sketchbooks are crucial to how I work,' she continued. 'I use them as "safe places" to draw out ideas and roughs repeatedly, often then scanning my favourite to use as final artwork. I rarely work in colour, preferring to work with a dip pen and ink, and layers of tone with ink washes, emulsion paint or soft pencil. I collect antique dip-pen nibs whenever I find them, and am always surprised and excited by the differences between one type of nib and another.'

Alongside illustrating the work of numerous writers and author-illustrating her own picturebooks, Smy has produced two highly successful and critically acclaimed novels, executed in an innovative combination of image and word: *Thornhill* (David Fickling Books, 2017) and *The Hideaway* (Pavillion, 2021). As a senior lecturer, teaching illustration at master's level, she has been a constant advocate of observational drawing and the use of sketchbooks as a way of building a personal visual language.

opposite
One of Pam Smy's quickly executed observational studies for *The Hideaway*, her part-visual novel from 2017, made in graveyards using inks and emulsion.

Pam Smy

Katrin Stangl

Katrin Stangl's strikingly bold, flat colour illustrations for her picturebook *Strong as a Bear* are perfectly described by the publisher of the English-Language edition, Enchanted Lion, as 'forceful in language, concept and colour'. The colours, produced as digital separations, are strongly influenced by Stangl's experience of screen printing, her dynamic designs making regular use of colour overlays and negative space. She also works in a range of other media, always experimenting with methods and processes.

Born in 1977, Stangl studied at the Academy of Visual Arts in Leipzig, Germany. A member for a number of years of the Spring art group, a Hamburg-based women's illustration collective and publisher of an annual print magazine, her creatively fearless approach to her work has led to numerous awards, including the Birkner Prize for Illustration and the Troisdorfer Bilderbuch Stipendium, one of the most important illustration prizes in Germany. Based in the city of Cologne, Stangl also teaches drawing at the University of Applied Sciences in Aachen.

'My sketchbooks are a place for treasure and trash. Looking through them, it is a little journey to the zoo, the museum, past projects, pictures I collected, ideas I already forgot and notes I don't understand anymore. I have a lot of sketchbooks. Our relationship is ambivalent. I do admire beautiful and well-composed sketchbooks, but mine are more the chaotic type. Sometimes started from both sides, including different things, no order, no dates. I admire artists who use them to sketch wherever they are, confidently, without any semblance of struggle, but it always costs me a bit of an effort to draw in public and I regularly take my sketchbook on holiday without opening it once. Nevertheless, I like and need my sketchbooks. Beside observation and all kinds of notes, they mostly include the very beginning of my projects. There are very rough sketches of characters, written ideas, sometimes tiny storyboards or experiments of material.

'They are like secret places, protecting all kinds of searches and failures until I find the right way for a specific task or text. But I'm not a loyal user. Mostly I'm shifting to white copier paper after some time, because I always feel comfortable to draw in the original size and with the option to throw things away easily. The sketchbook disappears under piles of single sheets, but – visiting an exhibition or getting a new commission – its time will come again.'

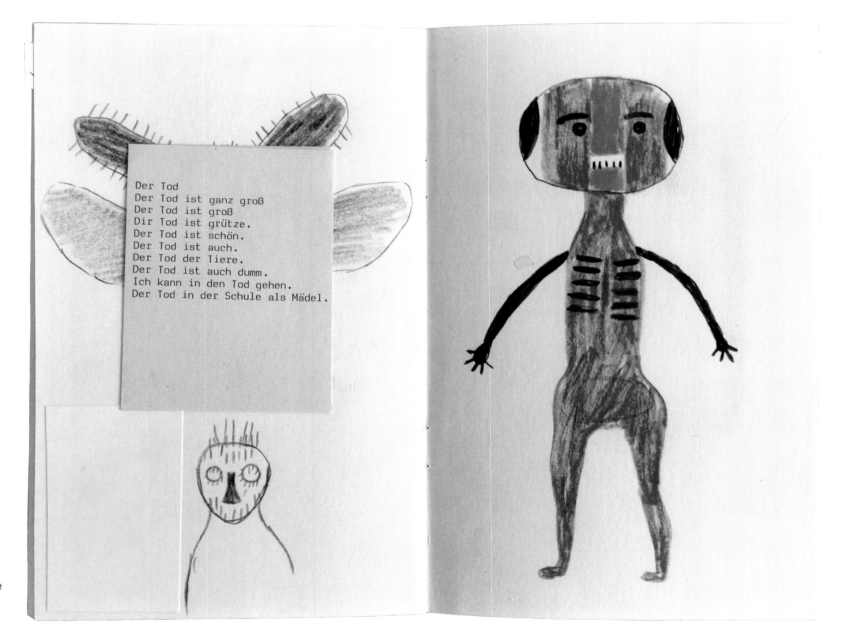

Der Tod
Der Tod ist ganz groß
Der Tod ist groß
Dir Tod ist grütze.
Der Tod ist schön.
Der Tod ist auch.
Der Tod der Tiere.
Der Tod ist auch dumm.
Ich kann in den Tod gehen.
Der Tod in der Schule als Mädel.

**opposite, right &
pages 252–253**
Katrin Stangl's rough,
linear sketchbook
drawings contrast with
the flat shapes of her
print-based work. Yet
they also demonstrate –
sometimes with an almost
medieval feel – the same
concern with order and
composition.

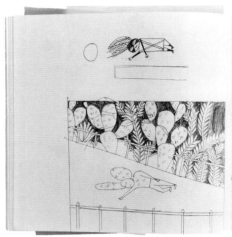
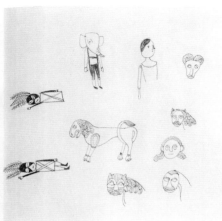
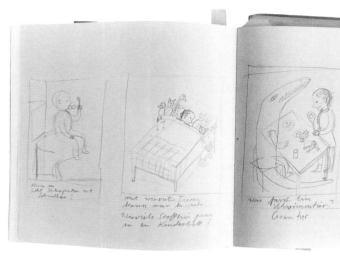
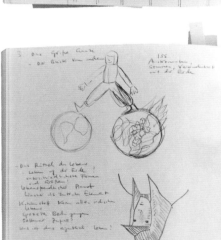

Illustrators' Sketchbooks

Katrin Stangl

Based in the north-east of England, Helen Stephens is an award-winning, bestselling picturebook-maker. Her work has been shortlisted for the prestigious Kate Greenaway Medal and, in the case of *How to Hide a Lion* (Alison Green Books, 2012), adapted for the stage. As well as producing her own work, she has somehow found time to establish the Good Ship Illustration, a thriving company that gives advice to aspiring illustrators.

For Stephens, the sometimes complex relationship between sketchbook and published work has helped shape her career. She originally studied at Glasgow School of Art, where she spent a good deal of time drawing from life in sketchbooks. Success soon followed, in the form of publishing contracts, but she was deeply dissatisfied with the work she was producing. As she explains below, this led to a dramatic change of course in an attempt to rediscover the importance of the sketchbook.

'When I first started in publishing, I thought, "Now that I am a *proper* illustrator, I have to get my head down and meet my deadlines. Playing in my sketchbook is frivolous." I couldn't have been more wrong. After a year or two of artistic direction from publishers, and no time for creative play, I felt bent out of shape. I wasn't enjoying my work anymore.

'I took a year out, determined to work out a bridge between my sketchbook work and my illustration, and find a truer voice. It was a nerve-wracking time. I lived on my small royalties, and lots of pasta and fish fingers.

It was during that year out that I met Fynn at Battersea Dogs Home, who became the dog in [my picturebook] *Fleabag* [Alison Green Books, 2014]. I worried publishers wouldn't like my new work, but the opposite was true. I think people can see when you are enjoying yourself; it shows in the drawing. Now I always make time for playing in my sketchbooks.

'Getting outside and drawing from life is like a magic reset button. If I'm struggling to feel inspired, I get out with my sketchbook. If it rains or snows, or I am feeling uncomfortable – even better. There's no time to overthink and the results can be unpredictable, which I like.

'When you draw from life, your drawing is at its most natural and spontaneous. So it's a good way to explore your own unique visual language. You can look back at your drawings and pick up clues: are you naturally loose and expressive, or are you more interested in design and placement on the page? I'm not choosy about the subject matter; I draw whatever's going on around me. I usually start with a few speedy, over-excited drawings, then settle down and relax, and eventually I get fed up and want to go home. But I don't, because I know that's when the good stuff happens. I don't put pressure on these drawings to turn into picturebook ideas, although sometimes they do.

'Some time ago I started the Instagram hashtag #walktosee to celebrate drawings made from life in a sketchbook. There are lots of drawings of people's kids, holidays, dogs, lots of domesticity and insights into people's lives, which I love – because I am nosy.'

opposite
Drawings from Helen Stephens's sketchbooks from her time as a student at Glasgow School of Art, made with the kind of fluency and freedom that she later feared losing.

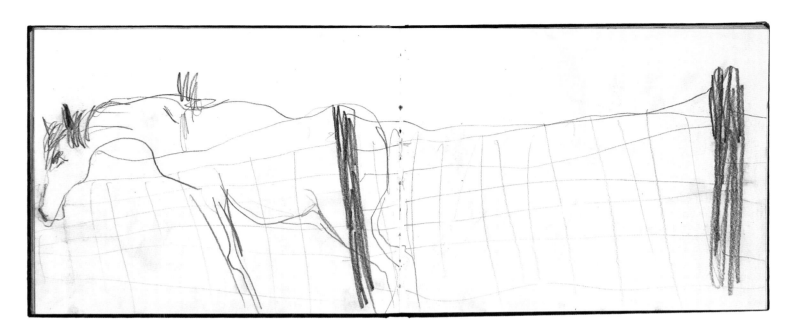

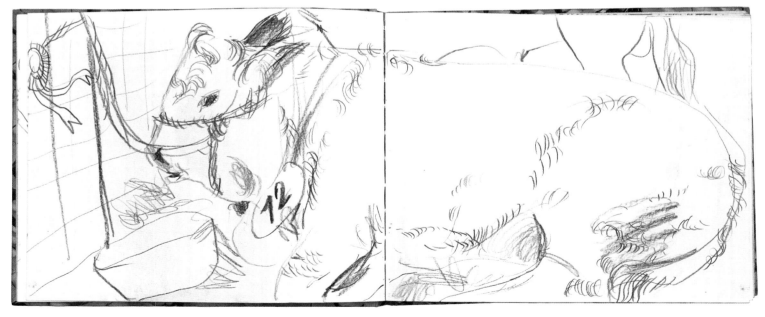

Helen Stephens

above
Helen Stephens's highly
successful picturebook
Fleabag began life as
sketchbook drawings of
Fynn in Battersea Dogs
Home in London.

opposite
In these two studies of
the small Scottish coastal
village of Burnmouth,
Stephens makes full use
of the landscape format
provided by her open
sketchbook.

Helen Stephens

Frieda making beans at stoneside hut April 19

Without doubt one of the superstars of contemporary graphic literature, Shaun Tan is a consummate visual thinker. He is also something of a rarity, able to fuse exceptional levels of formal, traditional academic draughtsmanship and painting with highly innovative approaches to visual storytelling for print. Equally impressive and similarly scarce are his ability and willingness to articulate in written form his working methods and philosophies, via his website and other media outlets. His essays, lectures and interviews, addressing the many questions that people ask illustrators (including the perennial 'Where do you get your ideas from?'), have contributed substantially to knowledge and understanding in a field that tends to be dominated by non-practice-led, literature-led theory. Here, he generously shares his extensive thoughts on sketchbook use.

'I sketch and draw in many formats, including small wooden panels for landscape sketches, large pieces of paper with pastel and charcoal for developmental work, and digitally using Photoshop. I also use sketchbooks in a variety of sizes, ranging from small Moleskines, able to fit in a back pocket and especially good for travelling, up to about A4 for desktop development and the rare occasion of a creative-development meeting for film or theatre.

'The choice of a sketchbook for me is twofold. Firstly, to keep ideas organized in one place. So a particular project will have its own sketchbook, used for doodles, writing and pasted-in cuttings; even digital images I prefer to print and paste. The drawings remain readily accessible, and serve as a memory device, as I'm inclined to forget much of what I write, sketch and cut out, especially on a big project spanning a number of years. It also avoids the problem of things getting lost in a messy studio, and mine is a messy studio.

'The second important function of a sketchbook is that it feels cheap, simple and unpretentious. That is, I never feel like I'm making anything so profound as "art" when working in a sketchbook; it really is just thinking out loud to myself, or testing to see what things look and sound like. I always buy fairly cheap sketchbooks where possible and usually work with simple biros. This further reduces any sense of doing important work, to not feel that it is serious or consequential, in order to keep one's mind free.

'My drawings in sketchbooks are, to my eye at least, typically bad, and sometimes bordering on illegible, like a doctor's prescription. There's usually just enough there to record a thought or figure out a visual problem, and I rarely revisit or edit any of it. It's all about moving forward, reacting spontaneously and process, process, process, not product. I also tend to sketch very small or lightly, which says something about the tentative nature of that process. No single line or word feels like a commitment; it's all just a quiet little test, almost a whisper that, if any good, I can amplify or translate later.

'Sketchbooks often graduate into dummies, or mock-ups of a book, which are a bit different but a continuation of process. Increasingly I put these together digitally for ease of editing, but in the early days I used to use a combination of photocopying, cutting and pasting, and direct drawing, pasted into self-constructed books. There are some examples here from the first book I both wrote and illustrated, *The Lost Thing* [see pages 264–265], where you can see this kind of patchwork development.

opposite
When working on a new project, Shaun Tan uses his sketchbooks to develop shapes and forms, sometimes using cut-and-pasted photos as a starting point.

page 262
Occasionaly, Tan will use his sketchbooks for a more developed kind of sketching. Here, he has drawn and painted around some found images that he has collaged together.

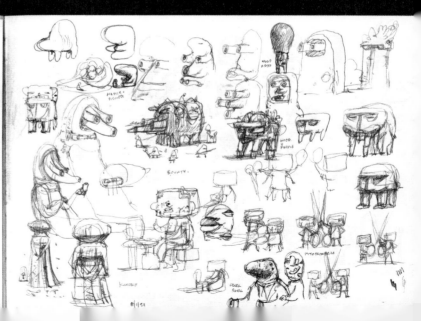

"FARM" TAN 5/1,

'My *Arrival* sketchbook page [right, bottom] shows a little of my process in "writing" using pictures, given that this is a wordless graphic novel. This is closest to what I mean when I say "doctor's prescription": they are the most basic kind of thumbnail drawings, purely for my own reference. Where the drawing is too cursory or risks being inscrutable later, I will add written notes for myself, to indicate what I was trying to draw. I think speed here is important, and not interrupting the flow of ideas with too much detail or revision, another reason I work with a ballpoint pen or pencil, and usually without colour. In this page, I was trying to plot out a sequence in which a young couple are escaping a genocidal attack in a fictional world. It's very similar to film storyboarding, a craft I've had some experience with as an animation director.

'The page here from my *Cicada* sketchbook [right, top] – a very small Moleskine – shows a similar process for a simpler picture book, about a lowly bug working in an office. Here, there is a combination of thumbnails and texts. Pretty much the entire book is represented on this spread, and other sketchbook pages show variations of the same thing – the whole story sketched out repeatedly as different versions.

'The pages "plant forms" [page 261, top], "creatures" [page 261, bottom] and "farm" [opposite] relate to a current project I am developing, which involves an imaginary ecosystem. Here you can see my use of cut-and-pasted photos – mostly from the Internet – as a basis for developing my own shapes and forms, a starting point for sketching. I find I always need to start with something, even if the sketching process goes in an entirely different direction; I can't really draw just out of my head very well. It's all about stimulus and response, and the

drawing then takes over in the sense that one drawing triggers another and another. The "seed" references I have used for this project are natural forms, typically tiny and microscopic organisms, as well as ancient stone and bone carvings, especially pre-Columbian art, for little other reason than I'm attracted to these forms.

The image "farm" [opposite] shows a page where I've collaged some found images together and drawn and painted around them. This is an uncommon example of the more developed kind of sketching I've produced within a sketchbook, as usually I will do this kind of work on a separate piece of paper or board. Of course, I could do this sort of thing all day but, alas, just don't have the time!

'The image "little plastic family" [not shown] is an example of a sort of mental ramble, this one loosely aligned with the project *Tales from the Inner City*, long before I knew the final form of that anthology – which was not like this at all. This one is a typical stream-of-consciousness sketchbook narrative that I will sometimes do if I have the time and inclination. In the past, I used to do this kind of sketchbook work often on long flights; for some reason my narrative imagination would be much more active when stuck in a metal canister in the sky. The story here is based on Margaret Wise Brown's *Little Fur Family* (1946), but where the characters are pieces of broken junk under a freeway, looking for beauty in their post-life, post-eco-crisis world, an idea I've never pursued but still like. I have a lot of these mini-stories in sketchbooks, which by themselves are not good, but I think could always be the basis for longer or simpler, more coherent stories.'

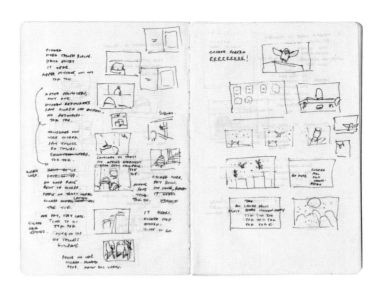

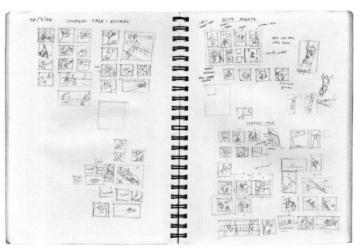

above
These spreads from Shaun Tan's sketchbooks show working notes and rough, early storyboarding for *Cicada* (top; Hodder Children's Books, 2018) and *The Arrival* (bottom; Hodder Children's Books, 2014).

below & opposite
Before digital processes took over, in the closing stages of a project Shaun Tan would mock up the final layouts in a sketchbook, using a combination of cutting and pasting, photocopying and direct drawing. The mock-ups shown here are for *The Lost Thing*, the first book that Tan both wrote and illustrated.

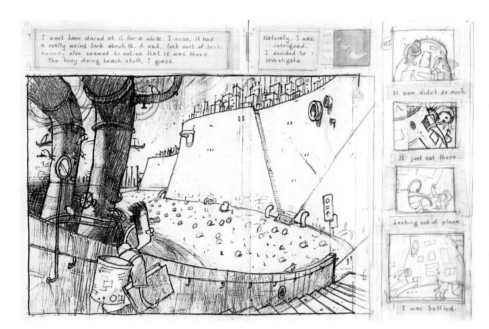

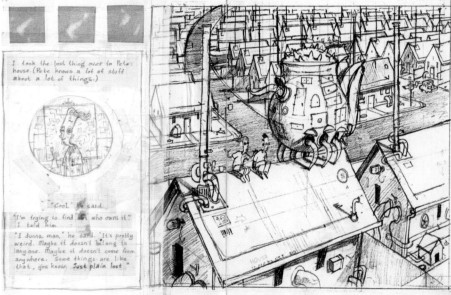

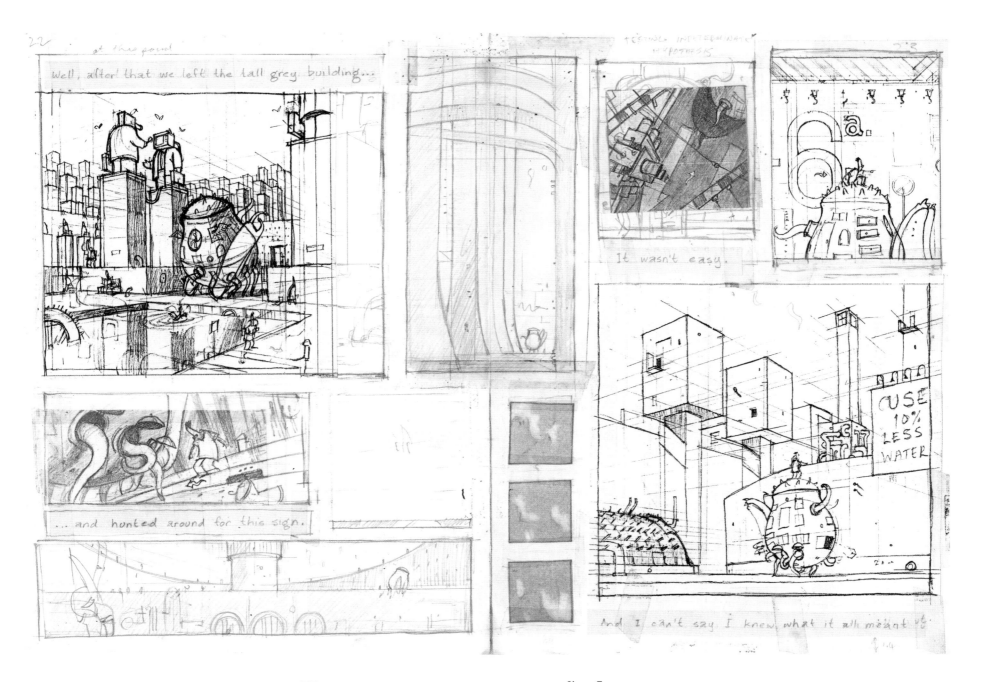

Shaun Tan

Victoria Tentler-Krylov

Born in St Petersburg, Russia, Victoria Tentler-Krylov now lives and works near Boston in the United States, having originally arrived in the country to study at the Cooper Union and Columbia University. As well as being a highly successful illustrator for magazines, advertising and children's books, Tentler-Krylov is an architect. The two interests came together in her 2020 debut as a picturebook-maker, *Building Zaha: The Story of Architect Zaha Hadid* (Scholastic). Other picturebooks followed, and in 2022 her work was given even greater prominence when she was commissioned to design her first covers for the *New Yorker* magazine. Her work has also appeared in the *Washington Post* and *Wall Street Journal*.

Tentler-Krylov's illustrations are often heavily populated by people going about their daily lives. Books that feature such compositions are often described as *Wimmelbuch*, a German word meaning, literally, 'teeming picturebook'. Perhaps the word *Wimmelzeitschrift* could be coined to describe her fabulously detailed magazine illustrations.

Like many illustrators, Tentler-Krylov now works primarily in digital media, using her iPad as a sketchbook. Here she explains how she became a convert to the practicalities of sketching on-screen.

'Having grown up with a pencil or a paintbrush in my hand since age two, I was

reluctant to even try drawing digitally. The sensation of holding a stylus or Apple Pencil and pressing it against the screen was awkward and felt like a weak approximation of the live hand-drawing process. But I believe in constantly trying new media and new techniques. I think it's one of the keys to growing as an artist. So, I continued to play with various digital sketching methods and interfaces, until I landed on Procreate on an iPad with an Apple Pencil.

'I started using it first as a way to quickly develop and revise sketches for final book or magazine illustration commissions, and then realized what a great solution it was for drawing, painting and sketching on the go.

Gone is the mess and the clutter of brushes, pencils, pads, clips and watercolours. And if one is as clumsy as I am, dropping or knocking over water jars is a constant occurrence. With the iPad, I don't feel like I've sacrificed anything – rather, the opposite. It gives me the freedom and luxury of having any painting or drawing tool at my disposal, including instantly collaging my photos into my sketches, which I do quite often.

'It goes without saying that my iPad comes with me wherever I travel, so I can sketch whenever I feel like it. It also comes with me to the beach, the supermarket, the subway and the local cafe.'

opposite & right
A series of quickly made compositions capturing everyday life in Prague.

opposite
Victoria Tentler-Krylov's
digital drawings allow her
to indulge her interest in
the activities of people at
work and play, unhindered
by too much equipment.

above
Two fully developed digital
illustrations, informed
indirectly by regular
anecdotal sketching.

Victoria Tentler-Krylov

For children growing up in Britain in the 1950s and 1960s, the wildlife drawings and paintings of Charles Tunnicliffe would have been very hard to miss. Many would have first encountered them via the seemingly endless series of Brooke Bond picture cards that were avidly collected by adults and children alike. Signed 'C. F. Tunnicliffe', the cards would be stuck into specially produced albums bearing such titles as *African Wild Life*, *Tropical Birds* and *Freshwater Fish*. Tunnicliffe's beautifully observed paintings of the countryside across the seasons were also to be found in the hugely popular Ladybird Books. While most of his young admirers would have been unaware that he had trained at the Royal College of Art in London and was a fellow of the Royal Academy, his work inspired many of them to venture out into nature and appreciate its diversity and beauty. It also inspired this writer to pick up a pencil, start drawing and, eventually, to study at art school.

Tunnicliffe was born into a farming family near the Cheshire town of Macclesfield in 1901. Growing up in this rural area of England, he developed a keen interest in the natural world alongside his love of drawing, the two quite naturally coming together. Accepting that he was unlikely to become a farmer, his family agreed to him attending Macclesfield School of Art. Later, at the RCA, he specialized in engraving and was quickly recognized for the finely detailed nature of his work, his prints soon being acquired by such international galleries and institutions as the Victoria and Albert Museum. It was perhaps his illustrations for the 1932 Putnam edition of Henry Williamson's hugely successful *Tarka the Otter* that first brought him to the public's attention. He would go on to illustrate more than two hundred and fifty books, both fiction and non-fiction.

Known for his trademark scraperboard technique when working in black and white, Tunnicliffe was skilled in a range of media, including pen and ink, watercolour, oil, and gouache. His collaborations with the writer Sydney Rogerson for the publishers Collins in the 1940s – *Our Bird Book* (1947) and *Both Sides of the Road: A Book of Farming* (1949) – are particularly notable. These lavish productions feature high-quality reproductions of the artist's drawings in the form of full-colour plates alongside dozens of exquisitely detailed scraperboard illustrations, all informed by Tunnicliffe's extensive knowledge of the subject matter. Although Tunnicliffe was always seen as a 'popular artist', these books especially stand comparison with the finest illustrated books of the twentieth century.

Tunnicliffe lived for most of his adult life in Malltraeth, a village on the Isle of Anglesey, off the coast of North Wales. Every aspect of his illustration work was informed by his legendary sketchbooks, which he filled with intensely observed studies of wild birds in their natural habitats – their movements, flight patterns and behaviour. The sketchbooks provide a fascinating insight into the foundations of his deep understanding of his subject through drawing. Some of them were later collected by the writer Ian Niall and published as *A Sketchbook of Birds* by Victor Gollancz in 1979, the year in which Tunnicliffe died.

Speaking on the BBC television programme *True to Nature*, Tunnicliffe described the role of the sketchbook in his practice as an artist:

'You must start from the live bird to get the life into your drawing. You take a sketchbook out and get as much of the live bird in it as you possibly can, and when it flies away from you, you go home and have another sketchbook, where you try to memorize what you have seen, and from these you possibly have an idea of the bird you want to paint. And you look at all of your information about the bird.'

opposite
In addition to his signature studies of wildlife, Charles Tunnicliffe produced detailed observations of habitat. Among them is this delicate view of Red Wharf Bay on Anglesey, the island he called home.

Sept 6: Red Wharf Bay. Evening light.
Wheat-field in foreground, with green crop on
right.

Charles Tunnicliffe

Sycamore tree near Llangaffo
Aug. 29 & 31

opposite
Another of Charles
Tunnicliffe's detailed
habitat studies, in this case
of a sycamore tree near
Llangaffo on Anglesey.

right top
Field studies of golden
plover in flight (left)
and golden plover
with lapwings on the
ground (right). The ink
line sketches on the left
retain the very brief
pencil under-drawing,
captured 'in the moment'
in just a few seconds and
clarified with ink later.
The colour study on the
right employs pencil, ink,
coloured pencils, and
dabs of yellow and white
gouache for the daisies
and buttercups.

right
Pencil studies of juvenile
guillemot at various
stages of development,
taken further with
watercolour washes and
white gouache on the
right-hand page.

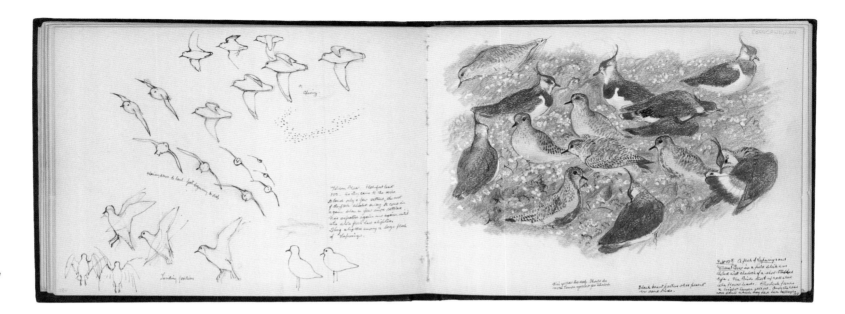

Tomi Ungerer's *Underground Sketchbook* was first published in 1964. Even as the Sixties were moving the world into increasingly liberated times, the explicitly sexual and, on occasion, dark nature of this private world must have caused considerable shock, coming as it did from an artist who had hitherto been best known for his brilliant children's books. He would stop making such books ten years later, to focus on adult themes, only returning to them in 1998 with the publication of *Flix*. But Ungerer had always been a nonconformist. He was a consummate visual thinker, a pioneer, a radical who used his art to challenge authority, intolerance and injustice, as well as to explore the darker aspects of the human condition. These traits and preoccupations are perhaps unsurprising given that Ungerer was born in Strasbourg in 1931 and, as a child, lived through the German occupation of his home region of Alsace, forbidden to speak in his native French and given a school project to 'draw a Jew'. His influences as a young artist included Saul Steinberg and other contributors of drawings to the *New Yorker* magazine. He moved to New York in 1957.

These images from *The Underground Sketchbook* cannot be given captions or augmented in any way by words or commentary. They speak in a language that is visual and direct, with economy and precision. They are funny, fearless, controversial, honest. As statements, they are so direct that there would seem to be little reason to make preparatory drawings; each line is searching and somehow both hesitant and knowing. Placement is crucial. In his preface to the original edition of the book, Jonathan Miller wrote, 'Ungerer has an excruciating inventive flair, cruelly comic, and those who read this volume as it should be read, straight through, in one sitting, will enjoy a sulphuric moral experience.'

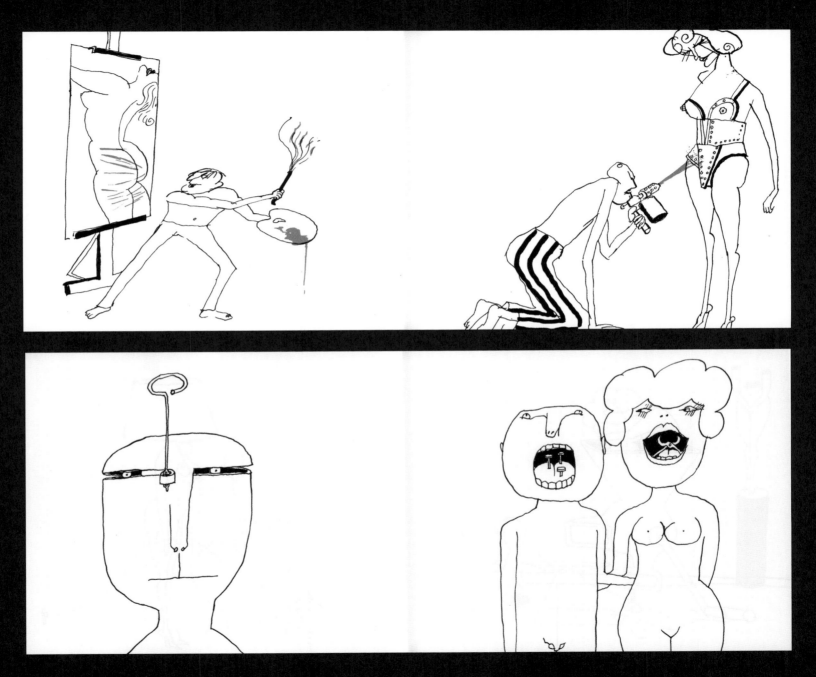

Tomi Ungerer

An ability to move from the densely patterned, verdant pages of such award-winning books as *Jemmy Button* (Templar, 2014) and *The Forest* (Enchanted Lion, 2018) to the sparse, designerly use of space in *Telephone Tales* (Enchanted Lion, 2019) is key to the flexibility of Italian illustrator Valerio Vidali's graphic art. As with Beatrice Alemagna, there is something of the 'innocent eye' to the work of Porto-based Vidali. That is to say, an element of child-like, naive vision in the mark-making that is paradoxically allied to a deeply sophisticated formal sense of design and of the process of translating the written word into the language of pictures. Vidali's approach to illustration also exhibits a highly developed understanding of the relationship between word and image and the potential for the artist to explore and exploit synergies between the two.

'As a general rule, as an illustrator, I always try to avoid drawing literally what the text is describing. I always try to "get away" from the text, in order to create a different, independent storyline that helps create a richer narrative.

'I always have two different types of sketchbook on my desk. A larger and thicker notebook, made with lighter paper, that I use often and carelessly, with a simple ballpoint pen or a pencil. This kind of notebook is an effective thinking tool that helps me quickly work out concepts and ideas. The other type is usually smaller and is made with heavier, higher-quality paper. I use this type in a later stage of the creative process, where I have already understood in which direction I would like to proceed, and I can focus on the aesthetic of the work, working out in full colour – most often with markers, inks or watercolors – aspects like composition, palette and technique. This type of notebook is usually the one that comes with me when I travel.'

Vidali has received numerous awards and accolades for his illustration work, including two appearances in the annual New York Times/New York Public Library Best Illustrated Children's Books listing and honours from the US-based Society of Illustrators and the Bologna Children's Book Fair.

below & opposite
Valerio Vidali has a keen interest in plant forms and often spends time in botanical gardens. Many of his illustrations reflect this passion.

Illustrators' Sketchbooks

Valerio Vidali

opposite
Two of Valerio Vidali's
sketchbook studies of
musicians.

right
Many of Vidali's
sketchbook studies feature
a kind of monumental,
sculptural approach to
drawing.

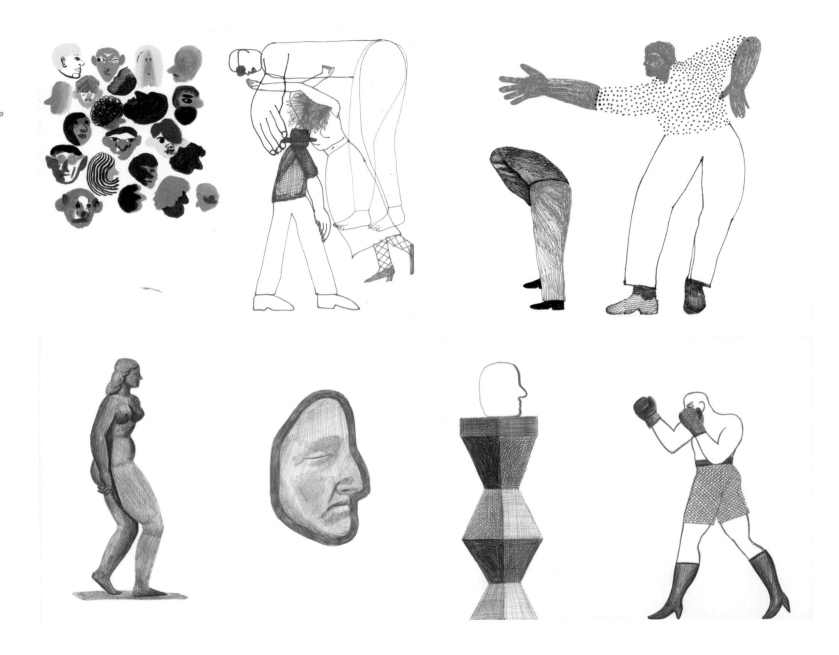

279   Valerio Vidali

Brian Wildsmith

It is clear from Brian Wildsmith's sketchbooks that he was a meticulous planner as well as a brilliant draughtsman. A proud Yorkshireman, he was born in the small market town of Penistone in 1930. His father worked as a miner, and Wildsmith displayed a talent not only for art but also for music and science. Eventually, aged seventeen, he chose to go to Barnsley School of Art, where he studied for what was then known as the Intermediate Examination, before gaining a scholarship to the Slade School of Fine Art in London in 1949.

The realist painter William Coldstream had just been appointed Slade's director, and Wildsmith found himself in a rarefied world of fine-art painting where how to make a living as an artist and support a young family was not part of the curriculum. After completing his National Service, he therefore decided to teach in a school while frantically visiting publishers to show them a portfolio of mocked-up book-cover designs that he had taught himself to execute. Commissions began to come in, but mainly for line drawings, as was the case for most illustrators at the time.

The opportunity to give greater rein to his natural painterly inclinations came in the form of a commission from the legendary Mabel George at Oxford University Press to produce a series of full-colour double-page illustrations for an edition of *Tales from the Arabian Nights,* which was eventually published in 1961. The commission was partly an experiment, to see whether an Austrian fine-art printer that George had discovered, Brüder Rosenbaum, could do justice to some picturebooks that she was planning to commission. The excellent results led to George publishing *Brian Wildsmith's ABC* the following year. An astonishingly bold, confident riot of colour, the book marked the start of Wildsmith's long and successful career as a picturebook-maker, and an equally long and successful collaboration with Oxford.

The desire to paint never left Wildsmith, and in later life, after many highly productive years as a bestselling author-illustrator whose books are loved around the world, he was able to devote more time to painting at his home in the South of France. Following his death in 2016, his sketchbooks passed into the care of his family. As is so often the case, they provide a fascinating insight into the thinking behind the more familiar, public-facing work – in Wildsmith's case, a world of painterly colour on the page. The sketchbooks are mostly devoted to the structural planning of his picturebooks: simple but carefully resolved compositions rendered in pencil at small scale, and focused primarily on the rhythm and pace of the picturebooks, building the foundations for each image but avoiding excessive detail, thereby leaving plenty of room for expressive exploration within the final colour artwork.

opposite
A page from one of Brian Wildsmith's large-format sketchbooks, executed while on a trip to Japan. Throughout his career, Wildsmith had close connections with the country, where his work was greatly admired and widely published.

page 282
These sketchbook pages are thought to relate to an unpublished Christmas-story project.

page 283
Some of Wildsmith's preparatory drawings for his illustrations to *The Snow Country Prince* by Daisaku Ikeda (Oxford University Press, 1990).

Rainbow

whole mountain of
Triangular trees

Tree wrapped
with straw
around
Trunk

Japan 9.10.89
Wildsmith

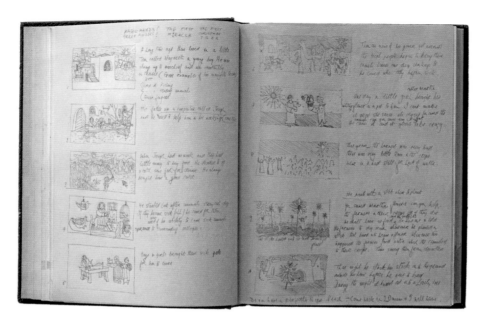

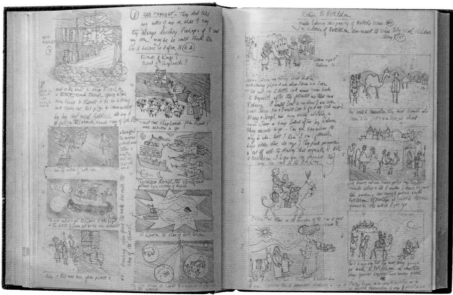

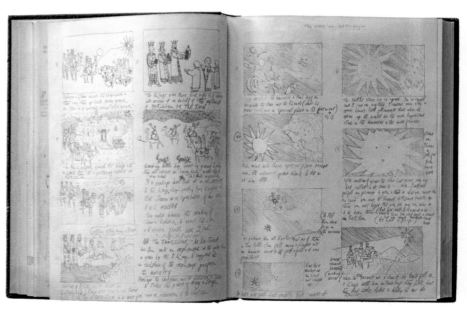

Brian Wildsmith

Peng Wu is a young Chinese illustrator whose work has been selected twice for the highly competitive Bologna Children's Book Fair Illustrators Exhibition, as well as being shortlisted three times for the Golden Pinwheel Young Illustrators Competition, part of the China Shanghai International Children's Book Fair. Based in Beijing, Wu works for a range of clients – both in China and overseas – in such fields as children's publishing, advertising and design; she also works for major national cultural organizations, including Emperor Qinshihuang's Mausoleum Site Museum. Her images are characterized by a genuinely child-like playfulness, full of natural warmth and interest in all human life.

For her senior middle-school years, Wu studied at Beijing Art and Design School, where, alongside traditional design and crafts, she was mainly taught the basic skills of painting. She then studied, at both undergraduate and postgraduate level, at Taiyuan University of Technology in Shanxi Province, majoring in graphic design. Here she begins by explaining that, despite receiving little tuition in illustration at university, it was her foremost passion.

'My heart was always in illustration, although I didn't then know that the kind of work I was doing at the time was called "illustration". Fortunately, I never gave up because I have always loved doing it. Since graduating I have been working with magazines, book covers, stationery, clothing brands and TV stations. When I was first selected [for the Illustrators Exhibition] at Bologna, I was just beginning to do children's books. That was also a time of cultural exchange between China and France, when many original works of Impressionism came from France to Beijing. Our school arranged for us to see the exhibition. That experience affected me a lot.

'The sketchbook is my best friend. No matter whether I am happy or depressed, it will always accompany me silently. I have many of them, lots of different sizes and with different paper textures. I decide which one to use according to the subject or mood at the time. And of course I choose tools that suit the paper. I like to record moments of inspiration in my life. That may be a scene in a movie, strangers on a journey, refreshing scenery, a delicious meal, some lovely plants, and so on. Any of them may become source material for future works. I also like to doodle aimlessly when I'm bored, starting from a simple random shape, drawing what I think or like and slowly expanding it into an amazing new world.

'When travelling, I like to carry a small sketchbook and some watercolour pens in my bag. When tired, I sit on the street or go to a coffee bar to draw. Sometimes I will stop to describe something that moves me, or draw the guests at the next table while waiting for dinner. These moments in time are pieced together into sketch after sketch. They don't need to be delicate or complete, it is just documenting what is around me, and it also makes the journey richer and more meaningful.

'When I don't have any specific project to work on, I will spend a few days painting in sketchbooks, choosing some rarely used painting materials and colours, drawing some parts or details, or topics that are not often involved, trying some new methods that I have never tried, and hoping for breakthroughs in painting. Of course, sometimes the results are unsatisfactory, but I think the process of the experimentation is more important. No matter what I draw in my sketchbooks, my original intention must be to draw freely and happily, without any

particular purpose or concern. Every once in a while, I will take out my sketchbooks and look through them. The pictures often remind me of the stories that happened at that time, and I can also see my progress in painting skills and changes in thinking mode at different stages. These are very precious to me. Sketching has become an indispensable part of my life. It happens naturally, gives me enjoyment and focus, and brings me great happiness and satisfaction.'

opposite, page 286 & pages 288–289
People feature as a subject in almost all of Peng Wu's sketchbooks. Whether drawn partially from observation or entirely from the imagination, they invariably convey a tangible sense of warmth and engagement.

page 287
In these luminously coloured studies, Wu allows the pre-printed blue frames of the sketchbook to lead her compositions.

MUSEUM

Peng Wu

26 · 3 · 2020

Peng Wu

29 3·2019 在意大利的 博洛尼亚慕塔诺拉
公园，这是我第一天到这里，顺便拍下了这
张照片给我。

peng wu
8 3 2020

想念大自
然，想念
海的味香
道。想棵
拥抱想
大树，想
抚摸松
的土软想
去壤，的
外面世界看看。

peng wu
7 3 2020

peng wu
17·4 2020

peng wu
18 3 2020

287

Peng Wu

Illustrators' Sketchbooks

Hello, Stranger
Sketch with Liuba in Ralph's coffee bar, Sanlitun Beijing
11·6·2021
Peng wu

　Peng Wu

Doris Meng Yan grew up in Hangzhou, China, and studied visual communication at the prestigious China Academy of Art. After graduating, she worked for two years as a visual designer and illustrator in motion graphics/animation before heading to the UK to take a master's degree in children's book illustration. Her debut picturebook, *Happy Chinese New Year!*, which introduces children to the many customs and traditions associated with the festival, was published by Lele Qu in China in 2021. A second book, *Mid-Autumn Festival*, followed for the same publisher in 2022. At the time of writing, Yan was working on a commission from publisher Thinkingdom to illustrate a Chinese edition of *My Special Day at Third Street School* by the Caldecott Medal-winning author Eve Bunting. In addition, Yan's lyrical, dream-like artwork has resulted in a number of awards and commendations in international illustration competitions.

'If I'm working on an illustration or picturebook project, a sketchbook is always the perfect place for me to go when I'm waiting for feedback, or sometimes just to change my mood. I can draw whatever I want and use different materials from the ones used in the project, and there are often unexpected things that pop up in my sketchbook! When I'm not working on a commission, my sketchbook is often my secret base for recording inspiration, exploring new characters, and drawing in different ways.

'I have several different sketchbooks: one for recording inspiration, ideas and reading notes; one with thinner paper for experimenting with coloured pencils and collage and for exploring different compositions and ideas; and one with thicker paper for watercolours and gouache.

Sometimes I copy and learn from the paintings I like; sometimes I just present my own ideas, and there are no rules or purposes.

'I prefer to use a single, large, thin sheet of paper as a sketchbook rather than a bound sketchbook, as it not only lays completely flat, but it's also easier to rotate and move around. Of course, the downside is that I often leave these sheets lying around, so they have to be organized by project or time period, otherwise they can easily get lost!

'I think that, apart from the final product, whether it is a commercial or a personal project, I use my sketchbook for all the ideas, thoughts and modifications from the beginning to the end, which gradually make up me and my work.'

**opposite, this page &
pages 292–293**
Meng Yan's 'sketchbooks'
consist of single sheets
of paper that she
retrospectively collates
by project or date. They
can be filled with highly
imaginative flights of
fancy, carefully considered
compositional studies and
observational sketches –
in no particular order.

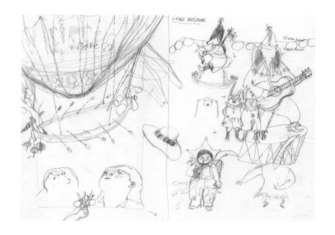

Illustrators' Sketchbooks

Doris Meng Yan

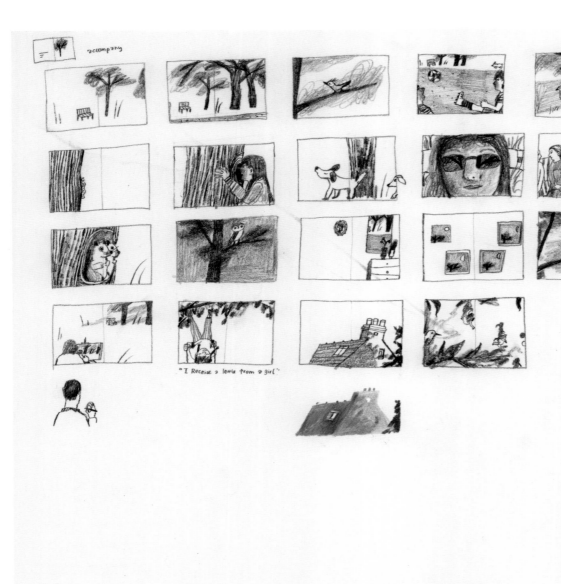

left & opposite
The complex mechanics
of picturebook planning
are revealed in these
exquisitely composed
storyboards.

accompany

"I Receive a letter from a girl"

- Not far from my home,
  there is a tree, a small tree that has not grown up
  there is a small hole in its trunk
  That is my favourite place
  I always wonder if anyone else found this place

- This little tree that has not grown up has always been
                                                    there
  Whether it is sunny or rainy
  day or night
  It's always there,
  stay with us.

- That little tree that has not grown up
  With the river behind it
  with the wooden chair beside it
  with the kite on its branch
  with the bright moon on its head
  with the window in front of it
  with the people around it

- We love it too   - And of course we will
  in different ways   always there with it
  to feel
  to record   Accompany this little tree that
                           has not grown up.

Leah Yang

Leah Yang is a young illustrator from southern China currently based in the UK, where she completed her master's degree in children's book illustration. She originally studied at the Guangzhou Academy of Fine Art, her education there consisting mostly of the more formal, academic grounding in drawing that is favoured in China. She went on to major in design, primarily 3D animation and graphic design, at the same institution. Yang found, however, that screen-based work was not to her liking, and so returned to traditional media during her master's. Her first picturebook, *The Polar Bear's Story*, is due to be published in China in 2023.

Yang has been drawing since childhood, having attended a specialist school with a strong emphasis on art. Throughout her education, she was taught to draw in a mainly realist manner – learning, for example, how to render complex formations of folds in clothing worn by models. As a result, she says, she is trying to forget or 'unlearn' some of these skills and recapture the eye of a child, revelling particularly in the instinctive, subjective use of colour, informed as much by emotional responses as by pure observation. Among the artists whose work she admires are Jockum Nordström, from Sweden, and Catia Chien, from Brazil.

Yang's sketchbooks demonstrate the draughtsmanship that was hard-earned during her years of academic drawing. They also reveal an ability to express colour through gestural mark-making in response to places and ideas. As Yang explains:

'I draw in my sketchbook rather like a cat under the chassis of a car, without worrying about who might see me. It is a safe and secluded place where I belong and I can do whatever I want. In the past, I used to spend money on more professional drawing tools and sketchbooks with better paper, but this often made me more hesitant and timid when drawing, fearing that the paper would be wasted if I didn't get the next "right" or "beautiful" line. It was often the cheap or even worn-out books that allowed me to concentrate on my drawing and feel comfortable. So now many of my sketchbooks are half-used notebooks.

'More and more of my "finished" drawings are now coming from sketchbooks, which may be scribbled and have many imperfections, but it does make them more attractive than my finished works. Thus, for me, the line between sketches and finished work is becoming increasingly blurred.'

opposite
A colour sketch made in the genteel English city of Bath. Yang brings the acute eye of the non-native to this loosely drawn observational study of ladies taking refreshments.

Leah Yang

opposite & above
Two studies made in the English seaside town of St Ives in late summer. Broad background colour was laid down first before being overlaid with pencil to pick out certain features. Coloured pencils were then used to add further detail.

right
Although she uses her sketchbooks primarily for observational work, Leah Yang sometimes jots down narrative ideas and possible compositions in pencil.

Leah Yang

left
A summer evening in Cambridge, England. Here, Leah Yang's direct, child-like and unselfconscious approach to drawing and painting helps capture the moment.

opposite
Working quickly *en plein air* with a keen eye for underlying compositional structure and pattern, Yang is able to convey a strong sense of the prevailing weather conditions and atmosphere.

233
Weidenfeld & Nicolson, 1969. All
images © The estate of Ronald
Searle

234–237
All images © Beatriz Lostalé

238–241
All images © Ana Sender

243–245
All images © Charles Shearer

247–249
All images © Pam Smy

250–253
All images © Katrin Stangl
www.katrinstangl.de
@stanglkatrin

255–259
All images © Helen Stephens
www.helenstephens.com
@helenstephenslion

261–265
All images © Shaun Tan

266–269
All images
© Victoria Tentler-Krylov
www.victoriakrylov.com
@victoria.krylov.illustration

271–273
Images courtesy of Oriel Môn
and by kind permission of the
Estate of Charles F. Tunnicliffe

274–275
Illustrations by Tomi Ungerer,
from Tomi Ungerer,
The Underground Sketchbook,
first published in 1964 by
The Viking Press, New York.
Copyright © 1968, 2023
Diogenes Verlag AG Zürich,
Switzerland. All rights reserved

276–279
All images © Valerio Vidali
@vidalivalerio

281–283
All images © The Estate of Brian
Wildsmith
@brianwildsmithofficial

285–289
All images © Peng Wu
www.illustratorwupeng.com
@_wupeng

290–295
All images © Meng Yan
www.mengyanillustration.
cargo.site
@doris_meng_yan

297–301
All images © Leah Yang
www.leahyang.com
@leah_wildpear

Acknowledgments

I am enormously grateful to the many people who
have made this book possible, especially the artists,
who have generously shared examples of their
sketchbook work along with their thoughts thereon.
Thanks, too, to the many artists' estates, copyright
holders and museums who have so kindly supplied
images and information. And finally, for their
incredible support and professionalism, special thanks
go to everyone involved in the book's production,
especially Mark Ralph, Ramon Pez and Ginny Liggitt
at Thames & Hudson; Maria Ranauro, the book's
picture researcher; and Therese Vandling, its designer.

Martin Salisbury is a professor of illustration at the Cambridge School of Art, where he designed and teaches on the renowned MA Children's Book Illustration programme. He has previously chaired the jury for the Ragazzi Award at the Bologna Children's Book Fair, and has served on juries for numerous other international illustration awards. He is the author of several books on the practice and theory of illustration, including *Children's Picturebooks: The Art of Visual Storytelling* (2012) and *Drawing for Illustration* (2022).

Front cover: © Oliver Jeffers
Back cover (from top): © Emma Carlisle (see page 58); © Bernd Mölck-Tassel (see page 198); by kind permission of Mick Marston (see page 192)

First published in the United Kingdom in 2023 by Thames & Hudson Ltd, 181A High Holborn, London WC1V 7QX

Illustrators' Sketchbooks © 2023 Thames & Hudson Ltd, London

Text © 2023 Martin Salisbury

Cover illustration by Oliver Jeffers
Interior layout designed by Therese Vandling

British Library Cataloguing-in-Publication Data
A catalogue record for this book is available from the British Library

ISBN 978-0-500-02330-3

Printed in China by Shenzhen Reliance Printing Co. Ltd

Be the first to know about our new releases, exclusive content and author events by visiting
thamesandhudson.com
thamesandhudsonusa.com
thamesandhudson.com.au